MAZI

MAZI

MODERN GREEK FOOD

**CHRISTINA MOURATOGLOU
& ADRIEN CARRÉ**

FIREFLY BOOKS

A FIREFLY BOOK

Published by Firefly Books Ltd. 2018

First printing

Publisher Cataloging-in-Publication Data (U.S.)

Library of Congress Control Number: 2017959534

Library and Archives Canada Cataloguing in Publication

Mouratoglou, Christina, author
      Mazi : revolutionizing Greek food / Christina Mouratoglou, Adrien Carré.
 Includes index.
ISBN 978-0-228-10034-8 (hardcover)
      1. Cooking, Greek. 2. Mazi (Restaurant). 3. Cookbooks. I. Carré, Adrien,
author II. Title.
TX723.5.G8M69 2018   641.59495   C2017-907193-9

Published in the United States by   Published in Canada by
Firefly Books (U.S.) Inc.   Firefly Books Ltd.
P.O. Box 1338, Ellicott Station   50 Staples Avenue, Unit 1
Buffalo, New York 14205   Richmond Hill, Ontario L4B 0A7

Printed in China

First published by Mitchell Beazley,
a division of Octopus Publishing Group
Ltd, Carmelite House,
50 Victoria Embankment,
London EC4Y 0DZ

Commissioning Editors: Eleanor
Maxfield & Sarah Reece; **Senior Editor:**
Leanne Bryan; **Senior Designer:** Jaz
Bahra; **Photographer:** Nicolas Buisson;
Chef & Food Stylist: John Skotidas;
Props Stylists: Laura Fyfe and Jessica
Georgiades; **Copy Editor:** Jo Richardson;
Production Manager: Caroline Alberti

TO TASOS, WHO
LOVED TO LIVE AND
MADE OUR DREAM
BECOME A REALITY

CONTENTS

INTRODUCTION

We opened MAZI in London's Notting Hill in June 2012 with a mission to change people's perception of Greek food. A culinary revolution had started in the capital and we felt that it was high time for Greek cuisine to shine and assume its rightful place in that transformative movement.

Up until that time, Greek restaurants in London had been stuck in the past with little creativity and innovation. As a Greek and a foodie, it always upset Christina that there was not one single place she could recommend to friends when they asked where they could find a good Greek restaurant. When we met for the first time, we quickly discovered we felt exactly the same way. Right then and there our idea was born — we determined to ensure that Greek food in London was given the chance to move on.

Adrien, French but born and raised in London, came from a business background in the restaurant industry and had worked for many years in different roles, from restaurant manager to fine food supplier; from wine importer to restaurant developer. But he had yet to realize his long-held dream of opening his own restaurant. Christina was born and raised in Thessaloniki, the culinary capital of Greece, among a family of foodies, and came to the UK to study and never left. Although her degree was in communication arts, Christina's love of food won her over and she ended up opening a small deli in Chelsea.

In this way, we both brought different things to the table that complemented each other — Adrien knew the London scene, while Christina knew Greek cuisine. What we both had a passion for was quality food and wine — and a good party! And together we wanted to share this love and our vision of a unique contemporary Greek dining experience with London's increasingly discerning restaurant-goers.

Finding the right venue is crucial when opening a new restaurant, so we were thrilled when we finally took possession of the former Costas Grill, a traditional-style Greek taverna from the 1950s, situated in the beautiful Hillgate Village. Adrien had been visiting this restaurant since he was a child and knew the owners. Even though it was five minutes away from Notting Hill Gate, it looked and felt Greek, with its own beautiful vine-covered garden — a rare commodity in central London. We couldn't have found a more fitting home for MAZI, as it perfectly embodied the metamorphosis of the old Greek cuisine into the new.

MAZI, which means "together" in Greek, references and revives Greece's noble sharing tradition, which lies at the very core of our ethos. We want to bring people together around the table for them to sample different dishes and flavor experiences, rather than being served a starter and a main course in the conventional way. But while we draw inspiration from customary practices and childhood memories, we reinterpret them with a modern twist. Another underlying principle of our approach to food is seasonality and we change our menu according to what produce each season has to offer. We also relish experimenting with sounds, sights and scents, as well as tastes, in order to offer our diners an all-round interactive and memorable experience. In essence, we want them to have fun.

Our dishes showcase the gastronomic delights of not just a single region but the whole country, from the Aegean Islands to the Peloponnese and northern Greece, which brings a rich variety to our menu. As you will discover, reflected in the recipes are the different influences exerted on the various regions by their geographic neighbors or historic events, most notably the 400-year rule of the Ottoman Empire and the Venetian possession of the Ionian Islands. Moreover, Greek cuisine has been fundamentally shaped by religious observances and festivals and national holidays through the calendar year which, for example, means we go vegan for the 40-day period of Lent in the run-up to Easter and we eat fish-and-chips on March 25, both a religious and historical holiday. And again, this has played a major role in shaping MAZI's menu. We strive to keep the taste of each dish as authentic as possible, but at the same time we play with its interpretation in terms of certain ingredients, its textures and its presentation — see our Cool Souvlaki on page 104 and our festive Melomakarona Tarts with Chocolate Ganache on page 223. Above all, we want each mouthful to transport our guests to Greece.

We feel very fortunate that customers and critics alike have responded so well to our new take on Greek cuisine. To have enjoyed such recognition and success in London and worldwide has been beyond our wildest dreams, and we owe a huge debt of gratitude to our loyal customers and the dedicated team who have worked so hard and supported us unstintingly all these years.

●●●

In this book, we are delighted to present the recipes for some of the most popular dishes we have served at MAZI over the years since we first opened, together with many of the traditional dishes that inspired them — always with a MAZI twist.

The majority of the dishes featured here are designed to be presented as part of a tapas-style feast. Serving quantities are therefore sometimes hard to predict and should be used as guidelines only as it really depends how many people you are feeding. We recommend always cooking a couple more dishes than you think you'll need. Trust us — this food is delicious and it will all go!

We insist on the freshest and in-season ingredients at MAZI and they can really make a difference to a dish. Where relevant, we have given notes on how to source any unusual ingredients and where these might be difficult to find, we have included suggestions for alternative ingredients.

We hope you enjoy taking this culinary journey around Greece as much as we did. Now go gather your loved ones together and start cooking!

Opposite (center) *MAZI head chef John Skotidas (left) with executive chef Alexandros Charalabopoulos (right).*

Below *Christina and Adrien in the courtyard garden at MAZI.*

An *amuse-bouche* is a single bite-sized hors d'oeuvre served at the very beginning of a formal meal, usually at Michelin-starred restaurants. While we can't boast a Michelin star at MAZI, we have enhanced this fine tradition in a unique way by giving it the Greek hospitality treatment and created the "amuse shot." Our guests are offered this shot with the menus as soon as they have sat down, not with the intention of intoxicating them, as it contains only a hint of alcohol, but just as a little taster to open up the palate for what's to come.

Our amuse shots vary according to the season as well as how we feel and what we come up with on the day, but we've selected four of our most popular recipes to give you an insight into the MAZI experience. Similarly, you can make and serve whichever of these fits the occasion as a fun way to welcome your guests, which is guaranteed to put everyone in a party mood and kick the evening off in high spirits. *Yamas*!

AMUSE SHOTS

PASSION FRUIT

3½ oz (100 ml) sugar syrup
   (see method)
1 oz (25 ml) mastiha liqueur
2 oz (50 ml) ready-made
   passion fruit coulis or purée
juice of 1 lime
3⅓ cups (800 ml) sparkling
   water or soda water

**MAKES 20 SHOTS;
1 X 1-QUART (1-LITER)
BOTTLE**

We like to serve this vibrant-tasting shot in the springtime. You can buy passion fruit coulis or purée from larger supermarkets. The purée is also available frozen online — this is the best type to use here if you can source it.

To sterilize the bottle for the sugar syrup, wash it on a quick cycle in the dishwasher and fill it with the syrup while it is still warm.

To make your own sugar syrup, gently heat equal quantites of granulated or superfine sugar and water in a saucepan, stirring, until completely dissolved and clear. Leave to cool. You can store the syrup in a sterilized airtight bottle in the refrigerator for up to 1 month.

Put all the ingredients in a clean airtight 1-quart (1-liter) bottle (ideally one with a swing stopper), seal and shake well, then chill in the refrigerator for at least 30 minutes before serving.

You can store the mixture for up to 3 days in the refrigerator.

WATERMELON AND MASTIHA

2–3½ oz (50–100 ml) sugar
   syrup (see above),
   depending on how sweet you
   want it, but we recommend
   using the larger quantity
7 oz (200 ml) watermelon juice
2 oz (50 ml) mastiha liqueur
4 mint leaves (optional)
2¾ cups (650 ml) sparkling
   water or soda water

**MAKES 20 SHOTS;
1 X 1-QUART (1-LITER)
BOTTLE**

This shot features Greece's famous mastiha liqueur, flavored with the aromatic resin of the mastiha tree (see page 241), which has become increasingly fashionable as a digestif over the last couple of decades. Paired with watermelon juice, this is a great shot for serving during the summer months.

Put all the ingredients in a clean airtight 1-quart (1-liter) bottle (ideally one with a swing stopper), seal and shake well, then chill in the refrigerator for at least 30 minutes before serving.

You can store the mixture for up to 3 days in the refrigerator.

Opposite *From left to right: Lime and Mint, Watermelon and Mastiha, Passion Fruit, Winter Orange and Spice.*

LIME AND MINT

3½ oz (100 ml) *tsipouro*
3½ oz (100 ml) sugar syrup
   (*see* page 14)
juice of 2 limes
juice of 1 lemon
6 mint leaves
3 cups (750 ml) sparkling water
   or soda water

**MAKES 20 SHOTS;
1 X 1-QUART (1-LITER)
BOTTLE**

This zingy shot stars the Greek spirit tsipouro, which is very similar in taste to Italian grappa. You can buy it from Greek delis or online, but if you can't find it, use grappa instead. This is a good choice for autumn. See the photograph on page 15.

Put all the ingredients in a clean airtight 1-quart (1-liter) bottle (ideally one with a swing stopper), seal and shake well, then chill in the refrigerator for at least 30 minutes before serving.

You can store the mixture for up to 3 days in the refrigerator.

WINTER ORANGE AND SPICE

3⅓ cups (800 ml) clear apple
    juice
3½ oz (100 ml) brandy,
    preferably Metaxa 5 star
rind of 1 orange
1 cinnamon stick
2 whole cloves
1 star anise

**MAKES 20 SHOTS;
1 X 1-QUART (1-LITER)
BOTTLE**

This is a warming, aromatic shot for serving through the colder months. See the photograph on page 15.

Put all the ingredients in a bowl, cover with plastic wrap and leave the mixture to infuse overnight.

When ready to serve, pour the mixture into a saucepan and heat to simmering point, then remove from the heat.

Pour into a clean airtight 1-quart (1-liter) bottle (ideally one with a swing stopper), taking care as the liquid may still be hot. Serve the drink warm.

You can store the mixture in the sealed bottle for up to 3 days in the refrigerator, gently reheating to serve.

Bread has always been an essential, everyday component of the Greek table, accompanying any meal large or small. Every street corner in Greece has a bakery that fills its surroundings with the heavenly smell of freshly baked bread, which is almost impossible to resist if you are walking by. Similarly, at MAZI we bake our own breads every day, offering them to our customers with Cretan extra-virgin olive oil for dipping, olives or our various condiments like *Tomatopeltes* (*see* page 34) and Kalamata Olive Cream (*see* page 35). Some of the breads, such as *Ladenia* (*see* page 25) and *Peinirli* (*see* page 31), can be enjoyed on their own, while other crusty, rustic breads are great for mopping up the contents of our jars (*see* pages 38–69) or for soaking up the juices of our Greek Salad (*see* page 74).

The following collection of recipes includes those for our best-loved and most characteristically Greek types of bread along with our favorite condiments.

BREAD & CONDIMENTS

KOULOURIA

9 oz (250 ml) warm water
½ oz (15 g) dried active yeast
1 lb 2 oz (500 g) all-purpose flour, plus extra for dusting
1¾ oz (50 g) superfine sugar
2 oz (50 ml) olive oil
¼ oz (10 g) table salt
14 oz (400 g) white sesame seeds

MAKES 10 RINGS

Pour the measured warm water into a small bowl, stir in the yeast until dissolved and leave to stand for 15 minutes for the yeast to activate.

Place the flour, sugar and olive oil in a large bowl. Add the salt to one side of the bowl and then carefully pour the yeast mixture into the other, ensuring that the salt and yeast mixture don't come into direct contact. Mix together to form a dough.

Knead the dough by hand in the bowl for about 10 minutes, or in a stand mixer fitted with a dough hook for 3 minutes on low speed and then 3 minutes on high speed, until firm and slightly sticky. Leave to rest for 15 minutes.

Preheat the oven to 475°F (240°C) or as high as it will go. Line 2 large baking sheets with parchment paper.

Divide the dough into 10 pieces. Shape one piece of the dough into a rope about 16 inches (40 cm) long, then press the ends of the rope together so that it forms a ring. Repeat with the remaining dough pieces.

Fill a bowl large enough to accommodate a dough ring with warm water and a second bowl with the sesame seeds. Dip each dough ring first in the warm water and then immediately in the sesame seeds so that it is well coated in the seeds.

Place the rings on the lined baking sheets and leave them to rise in a warm place for 15 minutes. Bake for 10 minutes until golden brown. Serve warm or at room temperature.

These sesame-coated bread rings are a very popular street food, orginating from the town of Thessaloniki (Christina's hometown), which is renowned for making the best koulouria. You can enjoy them for breakfast with a piece of cheese and honey or as a crunchy alternative to bread. We serve these at the restaurant as part of our bread basket.

TRY THESE WITH KASSERI CHEESE.

KALAMATA OLIVE BREAD

This is one of our most popular breads, and it really tastes of the Mediterranean. Dip it into extra-virgin olive oil, eat it with tarama (see page 50) or tzatziki (see page 51) or use it to soak up all the juices of your Greek Salad (see page 74). See the photograph on pages 26–7.

7 oz (200 ml) olive oil, plus
   a little extra for sautéeing
   the onion
1 large onion, finely chopped
2 lb 4 oz (1 kg) all-purpose flour
2 tablespoons dried active
   yeast
2½ teaspoons (12 g) table salt
7 oz (200 g) pitted Kalamata
   olives

**MAKES 3 ROUND
LOAVES; SERVES 10**

Heat a little olive oil in a sauté or frying pan, add the onion and sauté over medium heat until soft. Leave to cool.

If you have a marble work surface, we recommend using it for kneading the dough, otherwise a large bowl is fine.

Combine the flour, yeast and salt on the marble work surface or in the large bowl and mix in enough warm water to form a dough, then knead until the dough is no longer sticking to your hands. Cover with a clean kitchen towel and leave in a warm place for about 15 minutes until the dough has risen.

Preheat the oven to 400°F (200°C).

Add the remaining ingredients to the dough and knead until evenly incorporated. Divide the dough into 3 pieces and shape each into a round.

Place your loaves on a baking sheet or sheets, cover again and leave them to rise for a further 10–15 minutes.

Bake for 30–40 minutes until browned and crusty on the outside. This is delicious served warm soon after baking, but the bread will also keep well to serve the following day.

LADENIA

This delicious bread hails from the Aegean Island of Kimolos and is topped with luscious ripe tomatoes and sweet onions along with a generous measure of olive oil and fragrant oregano. See the photograph on pages 26–7.

9 oz (250 ml) warm water
⅓ oz (8 g) dried active yeast
pinch of superfine sugar
14 oz (400 g) all-purpose flour,
    plus extra for dusting
3¾ oz (110 ml) olive oil,
    plus extra for oiling
2 tablespoons tomato purée
3 white onions, thinly sliced
3–4 ripe tomatoes, sliced
sprinkling of fresh thyme leaves
salt and pepper

to serve
1¾ oz (50 g) pitted Kalamata
    olives, halved
sprinkling of dried oregano

**MAKES 1 X 13 INCH
(33 CM)** *LADENIA;*
SERVES 4

Pour the measured warm water into a large bowl, stir in the yeast until dissolved and leave to stand for 15 minutes for the yeast to activate.

Add the sugar, a good pinch of pepper and then the flour, a little at a time, mixing with a fork, until the mixture forms a dough. Finally, add a good pinch of salt.

Knead the dough on a work surface dusted with flour for 10 minutes. Cover the dough with a clean, wet kitchen towel or plastic wrap and leave to rise in a warm place until it has doubled in size — the timing will vary, so you can only judge by eye.

Meanwhile, preheat the oven to 410°F (210°C).

Brush a 13-inch (33 cm) round baking sheet or pizza pan with olive oil and place the dough in the center. Press it out slowly until it covers the whole baking sheet. Use 2 fingers to make indentations all over the surface of the dough. Spread the surface with the tomato purée and season with salt and pepper. Then add the onions and season again, followed by the tomatoes, seasoning again. Finally, sprinkle with thyme leaves. Season again with salt and drizzle with the olive oil. Bake for 40–50 minutes until nicely browned.

Serve warm with the Kalamata olives and a sprinkling of dried oregano.

LAGANA

The most distinctive of Greek breads, lagana is a large flatbread traditionally eaten on Kathara Deftera, literally meaning "Clean Monday," the first day of Greek Orthodox Lent before Easter. Clean Monday is always a bank holiday in Greece when, according to custom, people head off for a picnic and to fly a kite. Since meat and dairy products are forbidden on the day, one of the most popular accompaniments for this bread is tarama (see page 50). Although you would only find this bread in Greece on Clean Monday, we love it so much that we serve it with our jars (see pages 38–69) on a regular basis. When sliced, its long, thin form makes it ideal for dipping into the jars and scooping out every last bit. See the photograph on pages 52–3.

1 oz (30 g) fresh yeast

7 oz (200 ml) warm water

1 lb 9 oz (700 g) all-purpose flour, plus extra for dusting

1 tablespoon table salt

1 teaspoon superfine sugar

1 teaspoon ground star anise

6¼ oz (180 ml) Muscat sweet wine

3½ oz (100 ml) extra-virgin olive oil, plus extra for oiling

2 tablespoons white sesame seeds

MAKES 1 LARGE FLATBREAD; SERVES 8

Crumble the yeast into a small bowl and add 2 tablespoons of the measured warm water, then stir briefly to dissolve the yeast.

Add the remaining ingredients, except the sesame seeds, to a large bowl. Carefully pour in the yeast mixture, ensuring that the salt and yeast are at opposite sides of the bowl so they don't come into direct contact. Mix together to form a dough.

Knead the dough by hand in the bowl or in a stand mixer fitted with a dough hook until it is firm — how long this takes will vary, so you can only judge by the feel of the dough. Transfer to a clean, lightly oiled large bowl, cover with plastic wrap and leave the dough to rise in a warm place for 30–40 minutes until it has doubled in size.

When the dough is ready, flatten it and stretch it into a squarish shape no thicker than the width of your finger.

Place the dough on a baking sheet lined with parchment paper and use 2 fingers to make indentations all over the surface. Cover with plastic wrap and leave to rise for a further 20 minutes.

Meanwhile, preheat the oven to 375°F (190°C).

Sprinkle the dough with warm water and then the sesame seeds. Bake for about 45 minutes until the bread is golden. This is great served warm.

TIROPSOMO

Tiropsomo means "cheese bread" and is usually a type of fried bread made with feta, enjoyed in the morning or as a snack at any time of day. In our version we use a mixture of cheeses and give you the option of either frying or baking the breads.

Type 70 flour is a high-extraction flour, which means that it contains a high percentage of the wheat kernel ("70" denotes the ash content — the amount of ash that would be left after burning the flour, indicating a high proportion of bran and germ). If you have difficulty sourcing it, all-purpose flour is a suitable alternative.

Graviera is a pale yellow hard cheese with a slightly sweet and nutty taste, available from Greek delis or online, but if you can't find it, use Gruyère instead. Anthotiro, which literally translates as "flower cheese," is a soft mild cheese in its young form with a subtle floral, herby flavor, but you can use ricotta as a substitute.

11½ oz (330 g) type 70 flour
7 oz (200 g) white bread flour
¼ oz (10 g) dried active yeast
1¼ teaspoons superfine sugar
9 oz (250 ml) warm water
3½ oz (100 ml) warm milk
2 oz (50 ml) extra-virgin olive oil
1 tablespoon table salt
pinch of pepper
olive oil, for oiling
sunflower oil, for deep-frying

for the cheese mixture
4¼ oz (120 g) mature graviera
    cheese, roughly chopped
4¼ oz (120 g) anthotiro cheese,
    roughly chopped
3½ oz (100 g) feta cheese,
    roughly chopped

**MAKES 10–12
LITTLE BREADS**

Put all the ingredients, except the oils for oiling and frying and the cheeses, in the bowl of a stand mixer fitted with a dough hook. Mix on medium-low speed for 8 minutes. Add the cheeses and mix for a further 2 minutes.

Transfer the dough to a large bowl lightly brushed with olive oil and cover tightly with plastic wrap. Leave to stand in a warm place for an hour.

Cut the dough into pieces of about 1½–1¾ oz (40–50 g) each and roll them lightly with your hands into balls. Then using a rolling pin, flatten each ball into a round ½–⅝ inch (1–1.5 cm) thick.

Fill a large, deep saucepan no more than halfway with sunflower oil and heat to 340°F (170°C). Deep-fry the little breads, as many as will fit comfortably in your pan at a time without overcrowding it, for 1–3 minutes until golden on both sides. Drain and place on a plate lined with paper towel to soak up the excess oil.

Alternatively, shape the dough into larger breads, 3–3½ oz (80–100 g) each, and bake on 2 baking sheets in an oven preheated to 375°F (190°C), for 20 minutes.

Serve the breads warm or at room temperature.

PEINIRLI

One could argue that peinirli is the Greek boat-shaped answer to pizza. Besides our version, you can follow the basic recipe to make the dough and then create lots of different fillings by combining any other ingredients you like. You can also play around with the size of the dough base, shaping it into lots of little boats that are even better for sharing.

Pastourma or soutzouki are Greek spicy cured meats, which you can source from Greek or Armenian and some Middle Eastern or Turkish delis, but if you can't find them, use finely chopped bacon instead. Kasseri is a yellow hard Greek cheese available from whole food stores and Greek delis, but you can substitute it with Manchego, Gruyère or mature Cheddar.

MAKES 8 MEDIUM-SIZED PEINIRLI

for the dough
10½ oz (300 g) all-purpose flour, plus extra for dusting
7 oz (200 g) white bread flour
¼ oz (9 g) dried active yeast
1 teaspoon table salt
½ teaspoon superfine sugar
7 oz (200 ml) warm water
5 oz (150 ml) warm milk
2 oz (50 ml) extra-virgin olive oil, plus extra for oiling and brushing
melted butter, for brushing

for the filling
8 cherry tomatoes, quartered
7 oz (200 g) pastourma or soutzouki, sliced
10½ oz (300 g) kasseri cheese, grated
8 small eggs or quail eggs

Place the flours, yeast, salt and sugar in a large bowl, ensuring that the salt and yeast are at opposite sides of the bowl so they don't come into direct contact. Then add the measured warm water, milk and olive oil. Mix with a hand-held electric mixer on the lowest possible speed for 7 minutes until the dough is smooth and fluffy and doesn't stick to the side of the bowl, but make sure that it is still moist.

Knead the dough briefly on a work surface, then shape the dough into a round ball and place it into a lightly oiled bowl. Cover with plastic wrap and leave the dough to rise in a warm place for about an hour until it doubles in size.

When it has risen, remove the dough from the bowl and knead for a few seconds in order to deflate it. Divide it into 8 pieces and shape each into a ball. Brush them with olive oil and place them in another lightly oiled bowl. Cover again with plastic wrap and leave to rise in a warm place for a further 30–40 minutes.

Preheat the oven to 475°F (240°C) or as high as it will go.

Take the balls, one by one, and, working on a floured work surface, shape them into long, rectangular boats, like the hull of a ship, about 10½ x 5 inches (26 x 13 cm).

RECIPE CONTINUES...

Place 4 *peinirli* on a large baking sheet and use a fork to make a few holes in the center of each so that they don't rise during baking. Bake for 10 minutes.

Remove from the oven and reduce the oven temperature to 400°F (200°C).

Reserving half the filling ingredients for the second batch of *peinirli*, divide the other half between the *peinirli*, first adding the tomatoes, followed by the pastourma or soutzouki, then the grated cheese and finally cracking an egg on top. Don't overfill the *peinirli*, as they will fall apart during baking. Place the *peinirli* back in the oven and bake for a further 10 minutes until the cheese has melted but not browned and the *peinirli* are golden.

Remove from the oven and brush the *peinirli* with some melted butter to make the dough shiny before serving. Repeat with the remaining dough and filling ingredients.

GREEKS OFTEN EAT *PEINIRLI* FOR BREAKFAST, SO GIVE IT A TRY.

TOMATOPELTES

The inspiration for this recipe came from our grandparents' stories of Greece in the 1950s when workers were struggling to make ends meet. As tomatoes were always in abundance, tomatopeltes became the perfect spread for their bread and an ideal snack for their kids. It's healthy by default yet delicious on a slice of toasted bread, drizzled with olive oil and sprinkled with a pinch of dried oregano.

The recipe does require a big quantity of tomato purée, but you can buy it in 9 oz or 1lb 2 oz (250 g or 500 g) cans from Greek and Italian delis or large supermarkets. This is also great for using as a condiment to enhance sauces, stews or soups.

To sterilize the jars or bottles, wash them on a quick cycle in the dishwasher and fill them with the tomatopeltes while they are still warm. See the photographs on pages 26–7, 44–5 and 48.

1 lb 2 oz (500 g) tomatoes, halved and seeds removed
drizzle of extra-virgin olive oil
1 small white onion, chopped
1 garlic clove, chopped
2 tablespoons superfine sugar
good pinch of salt
good pinch of pepper
2 lb 4 oz (1 kg) tomato purée
18 oz (500 ml) soy sauce
4½ oz (125 g) honey
½ oz (15 g) flat-leaf parsley, chopped
¾ oz (20 g) chives, chopped
grated zest of 1 lime

SERVES 8–10

Grate the tomatoes into a bowl.

Heat the oil in a saucepan, add the onion and garlic and sauté over medium heat until softened. Add the grated tomatoes, sugar, salt and pepper and cook over low heat until the mixture has reduced to a marmalade-like consistency.

Transfer to a food processor or blender, add the tomato purée, soy sauce and honey and blend to combine.

Pour into a bowl and mix in the herbs and lime zest. Leave to cool, then transfer to sterilized airtight jars or bottles and store in the refrigerator. It will keep for approximately 1 week.

KALAMATA OLIVE CREAM

This is a great alternative to the standard olive tapenade for serving as a dip with bread. It's also good served with our Braised Octopus (see page 198) as a side sauce. See the photograph on pages 26–7.

10½ oz (300 g) good-quality
    pitted Kalamata olives
3½ oz (100 ml) water
1 tablespoon white balsamic
    vinegar

SERVES 8–10

Bring 2 different saucepans of water to a boil, then blanch the olives in each pan in turn for 5 minutes.

Drain the olives, then rinse with hot water. Add to a food processor or blender with the measured water and vinegar and blend for 8 minutes. Pass the mixture through a strainer for a finer consistency.

Store in an airtight container in the refrigerator for up to a week.

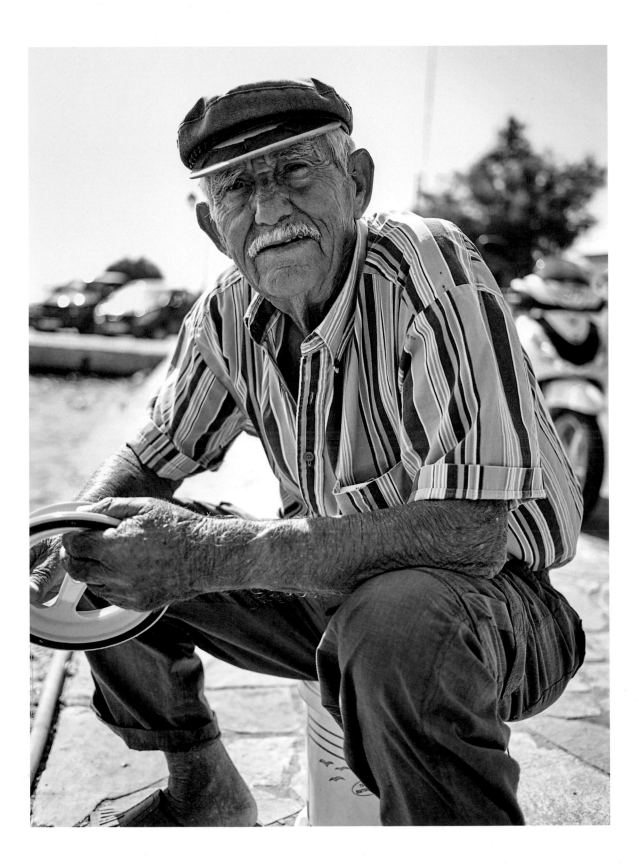

Every meal in Greece has to start with a selection of *mezedes*, or sometimes the whole meal consists only of *mezedes*. These are simply small dishes featuring a variety of ingredients such as meat, vegetables and seafood, a mixture of which is served with warm crusty bread and some ice-cold ouzo to sip. It's a sacred ritual that can last for hours between friends and family, talking and eating and drinking over and over again...

Our interpretation of this lovely tradition comes in the form of jars and we always recommend to our diners at MAZI to start their meal with them. At home, you don't necessarily need to serve these dishes in jars — you can use small bowls or plates. So here's a collection of our most popular choices from which you can mix and match. *Tarama* (*see* page 50), *tzatziki* (*see* page 51) and Grilled Eggplant (*see* page 40) or Santorinian Fava (*see* page 58) is a classic combination, particularly for the summer months, while *tiropita* (*see* page 42), walnut *skordalia* (*see* page 47) and Smoked Potato Salad (*see* page 65) makes a great lineup for winter.

The quantities we have suggested for each recipe vary, serving from 4 up to 10 people, depending on what else is served at the table. So just gather your loved ones together, in traditional *mazi* style, and enjoy!

JARS

9 large eggplant (3kg/
   6lb 8oz total weight)
4 tablespoons (60 ml) olive oil
½ white onion, chopped
1 garlic clove, finely chopped
5 ripe tomatoes
4 spring onions, thinly sliced
   into discs
1 small bunch of flat-leaf
   parsley, chopped
good pinch of salt
microgreens, to garnish

*for the soy and thyme honey
   vinaigrette*
3½ oz (100 ml) dark soy sauce
3½ oz (100 ml) extra-virgin
   olive oil
1¾ oz (50 g) thyme honey

for the balsamic vinaigrette
2 teaspoons dark soy sauce
4 tablespoons (60 ml) extra-
   virgin olive oil
1 oz (25 g) thyme honey
1 tablespoon balsamic vinegar

SERVES 8

This jar is without doubt
our all-time bestselling
dish. It has a distinctive
smokiness, a bit of
sweetness from the thyme
honey and a lovely texture.
Fans keep asking us for
the secret recipe. Well, it's
simple, as you can see. Just
don't be scared to burn the
eggplant to the point where
they turn completely black,
as that's what gives the dish
its unique taste.

GRILLED EGGPLANT WITH SOY AND THYME HONEY

Using tongs, hold each eggplant directly over a high gas flame or electric burner on your stove, turning at intervals, for about 15 minutes until they are smoked, the skins are blackened and the flesh is soft inside. You can also chargrill them on a hot barbecue.

Leave the eggplant to cool, then cut them in half lengthways and spoon out the flesh into a colander. Leave the flesh to drain for at least 30 minutes. Chop the flesh roughly, but make sure there are no big chunks left.

Meanwhile, prepare the 2 vinaigrettes. Starting with the soy and thyme honey one, blend all the ingredients together in a small bowl with an immersion blender and set aside. Then repeat with the ingredients for the balsamic vinaigrette in a separate bowl.

Heat the oil in a saucepan over high heat, add the onion and sauté for about 1 minute, stirring, until soft but not browned. Add the garlic and eggplant flesh and cook, continuing to stir, until the liquid has evaporated and the mixture is a dark smoky color — how long this takes will depend on how much liquid there is in the eggplant. Add the soy and thyme honey vinaigrette and cook for a further 2 minutes, then remove from the heat. Tip the mixture into a large bowl and leave to cool.

While the mixture is cooling, cut the tomatoes in half and remove the seeds. Dice the flesh of 4 tomatoes and slice the remaining one.

Once the eggplant has cooled to room temperature, add the balsamic vinaigrette and gently stir together. Add the diced tomato, spring onions, parsley and salt, and mix well.

To serve, divide the mixture between individual jars or bowls and garnish with tomato slices and microgreens. Alternatively, this will keep in an airtight container in the refrigerator for up to 3 days.

SPICY TIROPITA WITH BROKEN FILO PASTRY, LEEK AND CHILI

Tiropita is a feta and filo pie so popular in Greek life that you could argue that a typical Greek person eats it every single day. We have them for breakfast, for lunch on the go and with our afternoon coffee, and they will always feature at a feast. Our version is deconstructed in a jar with some leeks and chilies added to liven things up. Once you break the filo and mix everything together, you enjoy just a delightful mouthful of tiropita, much lighter and less filling than eating it in the conventional way, so that you can sample other dishes without feeling stuffed. Metsovone is one of the most revered cheeses in Greece, a semi-hard naturally smoked cheese. You can source it from Greek delis, but if you can't find it, use smoked Cheddar instead. See the photographs on pages 41 and 44–5.

2¼ oz (60 g) butter, plus a little extra for sautéeing the leek
1 small leek, trimmed, cleaned and finely sliced
1½ oz (40 g) all-purpose flour
18 oz (500 ml) milk
14 oz (400 g) feta cheese, crumbled
7 oz (200 g) Metsovone cheese, grated
1 red chili, sliced, plus extra, finely sliced, to garnish
microgreens, to garnish
honey, to serve

for the baked filo rectangles
3 large sheets of filo pastry
1½ oz (40 g) butter, melted
black and white sesame seeds, for sprinkling

SERVES 6

Preheat the oven to 410°F (210°C). Line a baking sheet with parchment paper.

Lay the 3 sheets of filo pastry on a work surface. Brush one of them generously on each side with melted butter. Place the second sheet on top of the first and brush the top with melted butter. Repeat with the third sheet. Cut the sheets into 6 rectangles about 6 x 3¼ inches (15 x 8 cm), cutting through all three sheets. Sprinkle each rectangle with sesame seeds, then place the triple-layered rectangles on the lined baking sheet and bake for 8–10 minutes until golden brown and crispy. Remove from the oven and leave to cool.

While the filo is cooling, for the "tiropita," melt a little butter in a small saucepan, add the leek and gently sauté for about 1 minute just until it is slightly cooked. Make sure you don't overcook it, as it will continue cooking once you add it to the cheese mixture.

Melt the remaining butter in a separate saucepan over medium heat, add the flour and cook, whisking with a balloon whisk, until a smooth paste (roux) forms. Gradually add the milk and cook until the mixture thickens, whisking constantly. Stir in the cheeses until melted and combined, then remove the pan from the heat, add the sautéed leek and sliced chili and mix together.

To assemble, divide the "tiropita" between individual jars or bowls and top with a baked filo rectangle. Sprinkle with a little finely sliced red chili, sesame seeds and microgreens, drizzle with honey and serve immediately.

RUSSIAN SALAD

As the name suggests, this dish (also known as Olivier Salad) originates from Russia, yet it has somehow become a quintessential feature of urban Greek cuisine. From the 1960s to the 1980s you could find it in every restaurant across Greece and beyond, as well as in supermarkets and delis. Still a beloved classic, it makes the perfect meze and also works well as an accompaniment to grilled meat, and to meatballs (see page 118).

4 large russet potatoes
4 carrots
5½ oz (150 g) frozen peas
6 small pickles, finely chopped
4 teaspoons capers
2 hard-boiled eggs, shelled
    and finely chopped

for the mayonnaise
2 egg yolks
1 heaping tablespoon Dijon
    mustard
9 oz (250 ml) sunflower oil
1 teaspoon freshly squeezed
    lemon juice
pinch of salt

SERVES 8

Start by making the mayonnaise. Whisk the egg yolks and mustard together in a bowl. Then add the oil a little at a time, whisking constantly, until you have a thick, glossy consistency. Add the lemon juice and salt towards the end of the whisking process and then whisk until well combined. Cover and refrigerate.

Peel the potatoes and carrots and cut them into large chunks. Cook in a large saucepan of boiling water until they are soft, but make sure you don't overboil them to the point where they collapse. Drain and leave to cool, then finely dice.

Bring the peas to a boil in a saucepan of water, then drain and leave to cool.

In a large bowl, mix the diced potato and carrot with the peas, pickles, capers and hard-boiled eggs. Add half the mayonnaise and mix gently, making sure all the ingredients are evenly coated. Then add the rest of the mayonnaise and mix well but gently.

This will keep in an airtight container in the refrigerator for up to 3 days.

SKORDALIA 2 WAYS

"If ever there was a dip to give hummus a run for its money, skordalia is it," declared chef and food writer Claire Thomson in the Guardian. Although traditionally served with battered fried cod on March 25, one of Greece's national holidays and most important historical days, there are different versions of this super-healthy dish and you can enjoy it with all kinds of fish and vegetable tempura, or simply as a dip with toasted bread. The first recipe featuring black garlic is a uniquely MAZI twist on the ever-popular classic, whereas the second interpretation using walnuts is a Mouratoglou family favorite with its distinctive crunchy texture.

Black garlic is available from some larger supermarkets, delis and food markets, as well as online, where you can also get squid ink.

...WITH BLACK GARLIC

2 lb 4 oz (1 kg) russet potatoes
4 garlic cloves, peeled
8 black garlic cloves, peeled
5 oz (150 ml) extra-virgin olive oil
2 tablespoons white balsamic vinegar
3 tablespoons squid ink
salt

SERVES 6–8

Peel the potatoes and then cut them into small pieces. Cook in a large saucepan of boiling water until soft. Drain well and leave to cool.

Blend all the garlic cloves with a little of the olive oil and some salt in a food processor or blender until smooth. Add the potatoes and then, with the machine running, add the rest of the olive oil in a slow, steady stream followed by the vinegar until the mixture is totally smooth and soft. Finally, add the squid ink and blend until well combined. Check and add more salt to taste.

This will keep in an airtight container in the refrigerator for 3–4 days.

...WITH WALNUTS

1¾ oz (50 g) stale bread (without crusts)
5 garlic cloves, peeled
pinch of salt
3 oz (80 g) walnuts
3½ oz (100 ml) extra-virgin olive oil
1 tablespoon white wine vinegar

SERVES 4

Soak the bread in water until soft, then drain and squeeze out the excess moisture with your hands.

Using a mortar and pestle, crush the garlic with the salt, adding the walnuts a few at a time and then the soaked bread, constantly crushing and mixing the ingredients as you go. Slowly drizzle in the olive oil and vinegar, working them into the paste gradually, until all is incorporated. If you don't have a mortar and pestle, use a food processor or blender following the same procedure.

This will keep in an airtight container in the refrigerator for 3–4 days.

BEET DICE WITH GREEK YOGURT, LIME AND CRUSHED WALNUTS

Super crunchy, healthy and refreshing, this dish is very easy to make and yet big on flavor. Besides serving with other jars as a meze, or with crudités or toasted bread for dipping, you could also enjoy this as a little salad.

1 lb 9 oz (700 g) raw beets
1 lb 10 oz (750 g) Greek yogurt
3 tablespoons olive oil
4 teaspoons red wine vinegar
1 garlic clove, grated
grated zest of 2 limes and
    juice of 1
3 tablespoons crushed walnuts
microgreens, to garnish

to serve
crudités
toasted bread

SERVES 6–8

Put the unpeeled beets in a large saucepan and cover with cold water. Bring to a boil and then cook over medium heat for 15–20 minutes, depending on their size, until they are cooked through and soft.

Drain the beets and leave to cool. Peel off the skins and then finely dice.

Mix the diced beets with the yogurt, olive oil, vinegar, garlic and lime zest and juice in a bowl, sprinkling the crushed walnuts on top before serving. To add a touch of contrasting color, garnish with some microgreens.

Serve with crudités and toasted bread.

This will keep in an airtight container in the refrigerator for up to 3 days.

FISH ROE MOUSSE TARAMA

Tarama is one of those popular Greek dishes that has been repeatedly transformed and abused, losing its essential character in the process. It's usually either too pink or too thick. Our recipe is different from the original as it's gluten free, and it has a natural color. The rule of thumb is that the better the quality of the fish roe and additional ingredients used, the whiter the tarama. See the photographs on pages 41 and 52–3.

3½ oz (100 g) fluffy-textured potatoes, such as russet

1 small white onion, halved and sliced into half moons

3¼ oz (90 g) smoked cod roe (white tarama), plus extra to garnish

4 tablespoons (60 ml) freshly squeezed lemon juice

1½ oz (40 ml) water

1 ice cube

14 oz (400 ml) sunflower oil

fronds of dill, to garnish

SERVES 6

Peel the potato, cut into large chunks and cook in a saucepan of boiling water until soft. Drain and leave to cool completely — this is very important.

Blend the cooked potato with the onion in a food processor or blender. Add the smoked cod roe, lemon juice, measured water and the ice cube and blend to combine. Finally, with the machine running, add the sunflower oil in a slow, steady stream and blend until the mixture has a soft, velvety texture.

To serve, divide the mixture between individual jars or bowls and garnish with extra smoked cod roe and dill fronds. Alternatively, this will keep in an airtight container in the refrigerator for up to 3 days (the more it sets, the better it becomes!).

THIS CAN ALSO BE GARNISHED WITH LEMON ZEST.

TZATZIKI WITH A HINT OF GARLIC

Refreshing, cooling, delicious and healthy, this renowned combination of cucumber and Greek yogurt is our idea of summer in a jar. Tzatziki goes with just about anything you can think of — bread, vegetables or grilled meat. And in our particular take on this Greek staple, we try to use as little garlic as possible.

This recipe makes a large quantity of tzatziki, but with all its varied uses, it will soon disappear! See the photograph on pages 52–3.

9 oz (250 g) cucumber
4 teaspoons table salt
4 lb 8 oz (2 kg) strained Greek yogurt
1¼ oz (35 ml) red wine vinegar
1 small bunch of dill, chopped
3½ oz (100 ml) extra-virgin olive oil, plus an extra drizzle to garnish (optional)
1 garlic clove, finely chopped
fronds of dill, to garnish (optional)

SERVES 10

Peel the cucumber, then grate into a strainer and sprinkle over 2 teaspoons of the salt. Leave to drain for a few minutes, then squeeze all the liquid out — don't hesitate to use your hands for this.

Tip the cucumber into a large bowl, add the remaining salt and the rest of the ingredients and mix well. Cover the *tzatziki* with plastic wrap and leave to stand in the refrigerator for 30 minutes.

Garnish with dill fronds or a drizzle of olive oil before serving. This will keep in the refrigerator for 3–4 days.

LENTIL SALAD WITH PICKLED GINGER AND "LAKERDA" SHAVINGS

Lentils are a very important ingredient in Greek cuisine and are widely used, especially in soups and salads. This is our original approach to a classic lentil salad in which Greece meets Japan. Lakerda is a cured fish meze that is popular in Greece, but you can buy ready-dried, fermented and smoked fish shavings known as bonito shavings from Japanese stores and delis, and online.

1 lb 2 oz (500 g) Puy, brown or beluga lentils
1 bunch of spring onions, chopped
1 small carrot, peeled and finely diced
3 oz (80 g) daikon, peeled and finely diced, or radish, finely diced, plus extra radish slices to garnish
½ oz (15 g) pickled ginger
1 bunch of flat-leaf parsley, chopped
5 tablespoons (75 ml) extra-virgin olive oil
¼ oz (10 g) bonito shavings
salt and pepper

for the vinaigrette
5 tablespoons (75 ml) extra-virgin olive oil
2 tablespoons red wine vinegar
1 tablespoon honey

SERVES 6

Rinse and drain the lentils, then cook in a large saucepan of boiling water for about 15–20 minutes until soft. Drain and leave to cool.

Mix the ingredients for the vinaigrette together in a small bowl until the honey has dissolved, then season to taste with salt and pepper.

Once the lentils have cooled, tip them into a large bowl, add all the remaining ingredients, except the bonito shavings and the vinaigrette, and mix together well. Season to taste with salt and pepper, add the vinaigrette and mix well again.

Garnish with radish slices and, before serving, scatter the bonito shavings over the top, then mix them in just as you are about to eat the salad.

GEMISTA RISOTTO

Gemista is a beloved Greek dish consisting of vegetables stuffed with rice or ground meat in a rich tomato sauce and baked in the oven, and its taste is very much associated with summers and home cooking. Here we have revisited this traditional favorite and turned it inside out, as it were, to create a sort of vegetable risotto-type dish that tastes exactly like classic Gemista (see page 115).

1 lb 2 oz (500 g) Arborio rice

1 lb 5 oz (600 g) good-quality canned chopped tomatoes, or ripe fresh tomatoes, grated

1¾ oz (50 g) superfine sugar

3½ oz (100 ml) extra-virgin olive oil

1 small onion, finely chopped

1 large eggplant, finely diced

2 small zucchini, grated

½ green pepper, cored, deseeded and finely diced

1 large carrot, peeled and grated

2 tablespoons tomato purée

1 bunch of mint, finely chopped

1 bunch of flat-leaf parsley, finely chopped

SERVES 4–6

Soak the rice in cold water for 15 minutes. Drain, rinse and add to a saucepan with 3¾ cups (960 ml) fresh water. Cook over medium heat, uncovered, for 20 minutes or until all the water has been absorbed.

Meanwhile, blend the tomatoes, 10 oz (300 ml) water and the sugar together in a food processor or blender thoroughly until smooth. Pour into a saucepan and simmer gently until the mixture has reduced and thickened to a sauce consistency.

Heat the oil in a sauté pan, add the onion, eggplant, zucchini, green pepper and carrot and sauté over medium heat for about 15 minutes until all the vegetables are soft. Add the tomato purée and cook for another minute. Then stir in 3½ oz (100 ml) water and simmer until the liquid has evaporated and the mixture has thickened to a sauce consistency.

In a large bowl, toss the rice with the vegetable mixture, tomato sauce and the chopped herbs. This dish is equally good served warm, at room temperature or cold.

SOME GREEK YOGURT OR FETA ON THE SIDE WORKS WELL.

SPANAKOPITA IN A JAR

Our deconstructed version of spanakopita, the famous Greek spinach and feta pie, was one of our most memorable dishes when we first opened MAZI. It's a characteristic example of the contemporary twist on Greek food that the restaurant is all about and paved the way for the development of our Spicy Tiropita (see page 42). Before serving, break the filo pastry into pieces and mix it all together, then when you take a bite it really tastes like authentic spanakopita!

1 quantity of baked filo
    rectangles (*see* page 42)
7 oz (200 ml) extra-virgin olive
    oil
4 bunches of spring onions,
    chopped
4 lb 8 oz (2 kg) spinach,
    thoroughly washed and
    well drained
1 bunch of dill, chopped
14 oz (400 g) feta cheese,
    crumbled
salt and pepper

SERVES 6

Follow the method on page 42 to prepare and bake the filo rectangles but without sprinkling with sesame seeds. Leave to cool.

Heat the olive oil in a large saucepan, add the spring onions and sauté over medium heat until they are really soft and caramelized. Increase the heat, add the spinach with salt and pepper to taste and cook, stirring, until starting to wilt. Add the dill and cook for a few more seconds until the spinach has wilted. Remove the pan from the heat, add the feta and mix really well.

Divide the spinach mixture between individual jars or bowls and top each with a baked filo rectangle. Serve warm.

SANTORINIAN FAVA WITH CARAMELIZED PEARL ONIONS

Fava, not to be confused with fava beans, are yellow split peas mainly grown on the Greek island of Santorini, which give their name to this local speciality that has made it all the way from the fisherman's table to Athen's most prestigious restaurants. This creamy purée is a fantastic meze, served warm or at room temperature, and it also goes really well with Braised Octopus (see page 198).

1 lb 2 oz (500 g) fava (yellow split peas)
2 carrots, peeled and chopped
1 large white onion, quartered
8½ cups (2 liters) water
6 tablespoons (90 ml) extra-virgin olive oil
juice of 2 lemons
pinch of salt
pinch of white pepper
sliced crusty bread, to serve

for the pearl onions
good drizzle of olive oil
7 oz (200 g) pearl (baby or silverskin) onions, peeled
2 tablespoons superfine sugar
pinch of salt
1 sprig of rosemary
2 tablespoons red wine vinegar
7 oz (200 ml) red wine
¼ oz (10 g) unsalted butter

for the crispy fried onions (optional)
½ onion, finely sliced
2 oz (50 ml) milk
sunflower oil, for deep-frying
1 oz (25 g) cornstarch

SERVES 8

Rinse and drain the fava, then tip into a large saucepan with the carrots and onion, pour over the measured water and cook (covered or uncovered) over medium heat for about 40–50 minutes until really soft.

Meanwhile, for the pearl onions, heat the olive oil in a large frying pan, add the onions and sauté over medium heat until softened but not browned. Add the sugar, salt and rosemary and continue cooking until the onions are caramelized. Then add the vinegar and wine and boil until much of the liquid has evaporated and the residue is syrupy. Finally, add the butter and stir until it has melted and the onions are nicely glazed.

Drain the fava thoroughly in a colander, then transfer to a food processor or blender. Start blending on high speed, and with the machine running, add the extra-virgin olive oil in a slow, steady stream, followed by the lemon juice, salt and white pepper. Continue blending until the mixture is soft and smooth.

If you are making the crispy fried onions, soak the sliced onion in the milk for 10 minutes. Meanwhile, fill a large, deep saucepan no more than halfway with sunflower oil, or a deep-fryer, and heat to 400°F (200°C). Remove the onion slices from the milk and pat them dry with paper towels. Toss them in the cornstarch, then deep-fry them in the hot oil for under a minute until golden brown. Drain and place on a plate lined with paper towels to soak up the excess oil.

Serve the fava topped with the pearl onions, warm or at room temperature, and garnished with crispy fried onions, if liked. Accompany by some sliced crusty bread for dipping.

SQUID INK FAVA
WITH FRIED CALAMARI

Having tried out this quirky version of the traditional Santorinian Fava (see page 58) at MAZI, we found it quickly became a huge success with our diners. This approach is more appropriate for the summer months and makes a great meze to accompany a glass of ouzo or ice-cold white wine.

1 quantity of prepared
  Santorinian Fava
  (*see* page 58)
1 oz (30 ml) squid ink
sunflower oil, for deep-frying
microgreens, to garnish

for the fried spring onions
½ bunch of spring onions,
  cut into strips
2 oz (50 ml) milk
1 oz (25 g) cornstarch

for the fried calamari
3 baby squid (calamari),
  cleaned and cut into rings
¾ oz (20 g) panko breadcrumbs
pinch of salt

SERVES 8

Follow the method on page 58 to cook and then blend the fava with the other ingredients. Add the squid ink to the food processor or blender at the end and blend for another few seconds until it is well incorporated. Set aside.

For the fried spring onions, soak the spring onion strips in the milk for 10 minutes. Meanwhile, fill a large, deep saucepan no more than halfway with sunflower oil, or a deep-fryer, and heat to 400°F (200°C). Remove the spring onion strips from the milk and pat them dry with paper towels. Roll them in the cornstarch, then deep-fry them in the hot oil for under a minute until golden brown. Drain and place on a plate lined with paper towels to soak up the excess oil.

For the fried calamari, coat the squid rings with the panko breadcrumbs and deep-fry them in the hot oil for about 1 minute until golden brown. Drain on paper towels as for the spring onions, then sprinkle with the salt.

Serve the fava at room temperature with the hot fried spring onions and calamari on top, garnished with microgreens.

DOLMADAKIA
WITH WASABI YOGURT

Dolmadakia, vine leaves stuffed with rice, is a dish that most people associate with Greek cuisine, but while preparing canapés for a party, one of our chefs came up with this twist on the traditional approach. Guests at the party liked it so much that we had to put it on the menu.

Fresh vine leaves can be bought from Middle Eastern stores, Greek delis and some specialty produce markets, but if unavailable, you can use vacuum-packed ones instead.

9 oz (250 ml) olive oil
1 large onion, chopped
1½ bunches of spring onions, chopped
2 garlic cloves, chopped
14 oz (400 g) Karolina or any medium-grain rice, washed and drained
14 oz (400 ml) water
1 bunch of dill, chopped
½ bunch of flat-leaf parsley, chopped
½ bunch of mint, chopped
grated zest of 1 small lemon and juice of 2 small lemons
good pinch of salt
good pinch of pepper
10½ oz (300 g) fresh vine leaves

for the wasabi yogurt
14 oz (400 g) Greek yogurt
1 tablespoon wasabi paste
1 tablespoon lemon juice
½ bunch of dill, very finely chopped, plus extra fronds of dill to garnish
salt and white pepper

SERVES 6

Heat half the olive oil in a deep saucepan, add the large onion and sweat over medium heat until softened. Add the spring onions and garlic and sauté until soft but not browned. Add the rice and toss around for 1 minute, then pour in the measured water and simmer for about 10 minutes until all the water has been absorbed. Remove the pan from the heat, add the herbs, lemon zest and juice, and salt and black pepper and mix well. Set aside.

Wash the vine leaves well, then tear out the stems and the thick bases of the veins. Blanch the leaves in boiling water until softened. Drain and transfer to a large bowl of ice-cold water to cool quickly, then drain again and set aside.

Use some of the vine leaves to line the base of a deep flameproof casserole dish. Lay the remaining vine leaves out on a work surface with their bases nearest to you and place 1 teaspoon of the rice mixture in the center of each leaf. Fold the right and left sides of each leaf over the filling, then tightly roll from the base of the leaf towards the top.

Place the filled and rolled vine leaves on top of the vine leaves in the casserole, sitting them next to each other in tightly packed rows. Then place the rest on top, again in tightly packed rows. Add the rest of the olive oil to the casserole and place a large heatproof plate, upside down, on top of the rolled vine leaves so that they are held in place. Pour in enough boiling water to cover the plate, then cover the casserole with the lid and cook over medium heat for 15–18 minutes until the water has evaporated. Remove the pan from the heat, take off the lid and replace with a clean kitchen towel, then leave the *dolmadakia* to cool.

Mix all the ingredients for the wasabi yogurt together in a bowl and garnish with dill fronds.

Serve the *dolmadakia* at room temperature or cold with the wasabi yogurt on the side.

1 lb 5 oz (600 g) baby potatoes
sunflower oil, for frying
pinch of dried oregano
1 tomato, finely diced
½ bunch of spring onions,
    chopped
½ bunch of flat-leaf parsley,
    chopped
pinch of pepper
4 quail eggs
salt

for the dressing
4 tablespoons (60 ml) extra-
    virgin olive oil
2 tablespoons red wine vinegar

SERVES 4

SMOKED POTATO SALAD WITH QUAIL EGGS

Cook the potatoes in a large saucepan of boiling water until they are soft. Drain well and leave until cool enough to handle, then cut into quarters.

Fill a large, deep saucepan no more than halfway with sunflower oil and heat to 400°F (200°C). Deep-fry the potatoes, in batches, for about 1 minute until golden. Drain and place on a plate lined with paper towels to soak up the excess oil. Sprinkle with 2 teaspoons salt and the dried oregano.

Mix the oil and vinegar for the dressing together in a bowl.

Place the potatoes in a large bowl and add the tomato, spring onions and parsley. Season with salt and the pepper, then add the dressing and mix well.

Heat a little sunflower oil in a frying pan and fry the quail eggs, sunny-side up, to your liking. Drain from the oil and place on top of the potato salad.

If you have a smoking gun, divide the potato salad between individual jars and top with a fried quail egg. Follow the manufacturer's instructions to fill the jar with smoke, close the lid and serve immediately.

For this recipe we took our inspiration from a typical Greek potato salad, keeping to its basic principles but elevating it to a whole new level. If you really want to wow your guests, you can use a smoking gun to add a dramatic theatrical effect to your presentation.

BARBOUNOFASOULA

This dish is a colorful combination of borlotti beans, tomatoes and herbs. In Greece, we call borlotti beans red mullet beans because of their red hue and we only eat them during the summer when they are fresh. However, since the beans are widely available dried, you can enjoy them all year round, and they are an excellent source of protein, fiber and vitamins.

1 lb 2 oz (500 g) dried borlotti beans

4–5 tablespoons of extra-virgin olive oil, to taste

1 onion, grated or finely chopped

14 oz (400 g) ripe tomatoes, grated, or 14 oz (400 g) can good-quality chopped tomatoes

1 tablespoon tomato purée

2 red Romano peppers, cored, deseeded and finely chopped

1 bunch of flat-leaf parsley, finely chopped, plus extra to garnish

2 pinches of superfine sugar

17 oz (475 ml) hot water

salt and pepper

SERVES 6

Soak the borlotti beans in plenty of cold water for 7 hours, or overnight. Drain and rinse.

Heat the oil in a flameproof casserole dish, add the onion and briefly sauté over medium heat. Add the tomatoes, tomato purée, red peppers, parsley and sugar and mix well. Stir in the beans and season to taste with salt and pepper, then add the measured hot water.

Cover the casserole with the lid and cook over low heat for about 40–50 minutes or until the beans are soft and only a little sauce remains. Depending on the quality and age of the beans, you may have to add extra water and cook for longer.

Serve the beans warm or at room temperature, garnished with extra chopped flat-leaf parsley.

Due to the favorable climate and fertile soil, salad and other vegetables in Greece are among the best in the world. So it's hardly surprising that our cuisine is rich in salads and vegetable dishes. Salad is an essential element of every meal, and it's rare to encounter a Greek table without one.

We Greeks love curing and preserving our fish and seafood, a tradition that has survived from ancient times to the present day, and it's considered the best meze to serve with ouzo. Fish is also enjoyed raw straight from the sea, lightly dressed or marinated, and there are many options to sample, from sardines to anchovies and from bonito to mackerel, as well as that shellfish classic, oysters.

Salads and raw or cured seafood are always served with *mezedes* or jars (*see* pages 38–69), before the meal moves on to hot plates (*see* pages 98–159).

SALADS & RAW

CURED MACKEREL WITH CAULIFLOWER COUSCOUS SALAD

Cured mackerel is traditionally served in Greek tavernas with crunchy raw onions, a handful of parsley and lots of freshly squeezed lemon juice. We have accompanied the fish instead with a raw cauliflower couscous, with the same contrasting crunchiness as the raw onions but turning a simple meze into a salad dish. In the restaurant we like to serve this with cauliflower purée and squid ink but it tastes just as nice without.

2 mackerel, cleaned, gutted and filleted but skin on
generous pinch of sea salt
1 tablespoon freshly ground black pepper
juice of 2 large juicy lemons
2 bunches of dill

for the cauliflower couscous
1 cauliflower, broken into florets
½ bunch of chives, very finely chopped
1 bunch of spring onions, finely chopped
½ bunch of flat-leaf parsley, very finely chopped
handful of raisins
grated zest of ½ orange
salt
handful of carrot leaves, chopped, to garnish

for the vinaigrette
5½ oz (160 ml) extra-virgin olive oil
3 tablespoons white wine vinegar
1 tablespoon honey

SERVES 4

Place the mackerel fillets in a glass food container with a lid and sprinkle them with the sea salt and pepper. Pour over the lemon juice and cover them with the sprigs of dill. Cover the container with the lid and leave the mackerel to marinate in the refrigerator for 3–4 days. Ideally, place a heavy object on top of the container so that the container is thoroughly sealed.

When your mackerel has been cured, make the cauliflower couscous salad. Reserving a couple of florets for the garnish, place the remaining cauliflower in a food processor and pulse repeatedly until it resembles traditional couscous. Pour into a large bowl and mix with all the other couscous ingredients, except the carrot leaves. Season to taste with salt.

Mix the ingredients for the vinaigrette together in a small bowl until the honey has dissolved. Pour the vinaigrette over the cauliflower salad and mix well.

To serve, divide the salad between the plates and garnish with the chopped carrot leaves. Place the mackerel fillets on top. Slice the reserved cauliflower florets and garnish each serving with a couple of slices.

GREEK SALAD WITH BABY PLUM TOMATOES AND CRETAN BARLEY RUSKS

What makes a good Greek salad lies in the quality of the produce and the balance of the seasoning. It's important to be quite generous with your dressing and to roll your sleeves up and mix everything together with your hands. This way, all the natural juices are released from the ingredients and the result is finger licking!

Cretan barley rusks are made from wholegrain barley flour, water and salt, and are super crisp and super healthy. You will find them in Greek delis or source them online.

1 small red onion, peeled
½ cucumber or 1 small
   cucumber, peeled
1 long green pepper, ideally,
   or ½ green pepper, cored
   and deseeded
20 ripe baby plum tomatoes,
   halved
a few capers
a few Kalamata olives
pinch of dried oregano
drizzle of extra-virgin olive oil
6¼ oz (180 g) feta cheese,
   crumbled
3 oz (80 g) Cretan barley
   rusks, broken into small
   pieces (or use leftover stale
   bread to make your own —
   see method)
salt
microgreens, to garnish

for the vinaigrette
5½ oz (160 ml) extra-virgin
   olive oil
3 tablespoons red wine vinegar
1 tablespoon honey

SERVES 4

Dice the onion, cucumber and green pepper. Add to a large bowl with the tomatoes, capers and olives, and season well with a good pinch of salt. Toss to combine.

Mix the ingredients for the vinaigrette together in a small bowl until the honey has dissolved. Pour the vinaigrette over the salad, add the oregano and extra-virgin olive oil and mix thoroughly, ideally using your hands.

Finally, scatter over the feta and rusks and garnish with microgreens.

If you can't find any Cretan rusks, use leftover stale bread to make your own. Preheat the oven to 400°F (200°C). Dice the bread, toss with some salt, pepper and dried oregano and spread out on a baking sheet. Bake until the bread is crispy — no longer than 10 minutes. Remove from the oven and leave to cool. They are then ready to use.

FOR THE BEST RESULTS, KEEP YOUR TOMATOES AT ROOM TEMPERATURE.

OYSTERS MOJITO

Over the past ten years, the Mojito has become the quintessential drink of the Greek summer. It was the intoxicating experience of sipping Mojitos at a beach bar in Mykonos and downing oysters straight from the sea that inspired one of our chefs from Mykonos to come up with this quirky recipe.

10 live rock oysters
microgreens, to garnish

for the sauce
5 oz (150 ml) olive oil
4½ oz (140 ml) yuzu juice
2 oz (50 ml) water
1½ oz (40 g) mint, finely
    chopped, plus extra to serve
1½ oz (40 g) Dijon mustard
pinch of salt
pinch of white pepper

to serve
1 red chili, finely chopped
1 tablespoon soft herring roe

MAKES 10

For the sauce, add all the ingredients to a large bowl and blend together with an immersion blender. Pass through a fine-mesh strainer.

Scrub the shells of the oysters thoroughly. To open, sit an oyster on a cutting board covered with a clean kitchen towel, flat shell up, and hold the rounded end of the oyster firmly with the kitchen towel. Insert an oyster knife or other small strong knife into the pointed (hinged) end just below the top shell, point the blade downwards and twist it from side to side to lever the hinge open. The hinge should pop open. Keeping the oyster level to avoid losing any of the precious juices, reach the blade further into the shell, running it close to the underside of the top shell, and cut through the muscle to release the oyster from the top shell.

Lift off the top shell and check for and remove any broken bits of shell or grit. Gently release the oyster meat from the bottom shell using the knife and carefully transfer to a small bowl with any juices. Wash the bottom shell and pat dry, pour some sauce into each shell and return the oyster meat. Add a sprinkle of chopped chili and mint to the shell and top with a little herring roe. Serve immediately, garnished with microgreens.

BLACK-EYED BEAN SALAD

Packed with both nutrients and flavor, this aromatic bean salad was inspired by the dishes that Greeks traditionally eat when fasting prior to the Orthodox Easter, and it brings spring to our minds. The dish can be enjoyed on its own, but it also combines beautifully with our Grilled Calamari (see page 187) and cuttlefish. See the photograph on page 186.

1 lb 2 oz (500 g) dried black-eyed beans
1 bunch of dill, chopped
1 bunch of flat-leaf parsley, chopped
½ bunch of chives, chopped
grated zest and juice of 1 large lemon
grated zest of 1 lime
1 roasted red pepper from a jar, drained and diced
2 spring onions, chopped
pinch of salt
drizzle of extra-virgin olive oil

for the vinaigrette
5½ oz (160 ml) extra-virgin olive oil
3 tablespoons red wine vinegar
1 tablespoon honey
pinch of salt

SERVES 4–6

Soak the black-eyed beans in plenty of cold water for a minimum of 7 hours, or overnight.

Drain and rinse the beans. Cook in a saucepan of boiling water for 1 hour or until soft. Drain and leave to cool.

Mix the ingredients for the vinaigrette together in a small bowl until the honey has dissolved.

Add the cooled beans to a large bowl with the rest of ingredients, except the vinaigrette, and mix together. Finally, add the vinaigrette and toss to combine. Serve at room temperature or cold.

STIR-FRIED POLITIKI SALAD

This recipe was originally introduced to our cuisine by the Greeks of Constantinople, politiki meaning something that comes from poli, which literally translates from the Greek as "city" but is also used to refer to Constantinople (now Istanbul). It's a very popular winter dish, normally served raw and cold, but one of our chefs had the brilliant idea of transforming it into a stir-fry. Try it as a side dish with our Filet Mignon Kontosouvli (see page 162) or Caramelized Iberico Pork Chop (see page 166). See the photograph on page 163.

1 white cabbage, shredded
2 long red peppers, cored, deseeded and cut into very thin strips
1 large carrot, peeled and shredded
1 celery stick, very thinly sliced
1 red onion, cut into very thin strips
drizzle of extra-virgin olive oil
drizzle of white balsamic vinegar
1 bunch of flat-leaf parsley, chopped
pinch of white sesame seeds
pinch of black sesame seeds
salt

SERVES 6

Mix all the vegetables together in a bowl so that they are well combined.

Heat a large frying pan or wok until very hot, add the olive oil and then stir-fry the vegetables for about 1 minute. Drizzle with the white balsamic vinegar and remove the pan from the heat. Add the chopped parsley and season with salt.

Transfer to a serving bowl and sprinkle the sesame seeds over the top. Serve immediately.

THIS GOES VERY WELL WITH MEAT AND HEARTY WINTER SOUPS.

SEA BREAM TARTARE

Sea bream is one of the many Mediterranean fish to be found in abundance in Greek waters, although it's also common in the Atlantic. Grilling is the traditional treatment for this fish, originating from the Cyclades, but preparing it as a tartare is the new trend that has taken over the country. One of our chefs from Mykonos has devised this distinctive version for MAZI.

2 medium-sized sea bream, cleaned, gutted, filleted and skinned (each fillet about 5 oz [140 g])
½ bunch of cilantro, chopped
1 red chili, finely chopped
2¾–3½ oz (80–100 ml) extra-virgin olive oil
grated zest of 1 lime and juice of ½
½ shallot, finely chopped
2 pinches of salt
pinch of pepper

for the avocado mousse
1 lb 5 oz (600 g) avocados (about 2–3, depending on size)
1 teaspoon chopped red chili
1 bunch of cilantro
juice of 1½ limes
pinch of salt
pinch of pepper

SERVES 6

Finely dice the fish fillets. Add to a glass or ceramic bowl with the rest of the main ingredients, mix together and set aside at room temperature while you prepare the avocado mousse.

Cut each avocado in half and remove the stone, then peel the flesh. Add to a food processor or blender with the rest of the ingredients and blend until creamy.

To serve, divide the avocado mousse between plates and arrange the sea bream tartare on top.

THE MORE LIME JUICE YOU ADD TO THIS, THE BETTER.

MARINATED HERRINGS IN VINEGAR WITH SEA ROSEMARY

So simple and yet so delicious, for us this is the ultimate meze, encapsulating Greece in a mouthful. You can use this recipe to marinate fresh sardines or anchovies in the same way.

As its name suggests, sea rosemary grows close to the sea and has a naturally salty aromatic flavor that marries well with fish. Look out for it at speciality grocers. If you can't find it, try using marsh samphire, available from large supermarkets.

1 lb 2 oz (500 g) herring fillets
17½ oz (285 ml) white wine vinegar
17½ oz (285 ml) extra-virgin olive oil
1 tablespoon sea salt
1 bunch of spring onions, finely chopped
1 red chili, very finely diced
a few sprigs of sea rosemary, leaves picked
a few flat-leaf parsley leaves

SERVES 4

Rinse the herring fillets and pat them dry with paper towels. Place them in a large oval glass or ceramic dish and drizzle over the vinegar. Cover and leave to marinate in the refrigerator for at least 8 hours.

Remove the herrings from the marinade and dress with the olive oil and sea salt. Sprinkle with the spring onions, chili, sea rosemary and flat-leaf parsley, and they are ready to serve.

FIGS, WARM TALAGANI AND BABY LEAVES WITH RAKOMELO VINAIGRETTE

Figs and talagani cheese were made for each other, while rakomelo is a traditional Cretan drink that consists of warm raki (pomace brandy) and honey. All these elements come together in this salad to create a great combination of sweet, salty and sour.

Talagani is a traditional handmade Greek cheese made from sheep milk and is best eaten grilled or fried when it acquires texture. If you can't find it, substitute halloumi or goat cheese.

14 oz (400 g) mixed baby salad leaves
4 fresh figs or 10½ oz (300 g) dried figs, stems removed and diced
1 pear, peeled, cored and diced
9 oz (250 g) talagani cheese
handful of hazelnuts, crushed and (ideally) toasted
salt

for the rakomelo **vinaigrette**
1 tablespoon Greek raki or tsipouro, plus an extra 4 teaspoons
¼ oz (10 g) honey, plus an extra 1¼ oz (35 g)
1 clove
small piece of cinnamon stick
3½ tablespoons balsamic vinegar
¾ oz (20 g) Dijon mustard
5 tablespoons (75 ml) extra-virgin olive oil
5 tablespoons (75 ml) sunflower oil
salt and pepper

SERVES 4

Start by making the rakomelo vinaigrette. Mix the 1 tablespoon raki or tsipouro and ¼ oz (10 g) honey in a small saucepan and add the clove and cinnamon stick. Simmer, stirring, until the honey has melted and the spices have infused the mixture.

Remove the pan from the heat and take out the cinnamon stick and clove, then add to a food processor or blender with the rest of the ingredients apart from the oils. Start blending on high speed, then with the machine running, add the oils in a slow, steady stream until incorporated.

Add the baby salad leaves, figs and pear to a large bowl and season with salt. Pour in the vinaigrette and mix well so that all the salad ingredients are thoroughly coated.

Cut the cheese into wedges and cook in a hot griddle pan or frying pan for a few seconds on each side.

Add the cheese to the salad and sprinkle the crushed hazelnuts on top.

LITTLE GEM AND CHICORY SALAD WITH DILL AND SPRING ONIONS

We regard this dish as the second national salad of Greece (after the classic Greek Salad — see page 74) and the essential universal accompaniment to roast lamb. Usually containing finely chopped lettuce, dill and spring onions, we have played with the original recipe, adding chicory to bring an edge to it. Drew Barrymore, since you asked us to give you the recipe, this one's for you!

1 little gem lettuce
2 heads of white chicory,
    cut into fine strips
2 spring onions, chopped
a few fronds of dill
salt

for the vinaigrette
5½ oz (160 ml) extra-virgin
    olive oil
3 tablespoons white balsamic
    vinegar
1 tablespoon honey
pinch of salt

SERVES 4

Wash the little gem lettuce thoroughly and separate it into whole leaves. Pat them dry and place them in a bowl.

Mix all the ingredients for the vinaigrette together in a small bowl until the honey has dissolved.

Add the chicory to the little gem lettuce and season with salt, then pour over the vinaigrette and mix well. Sprinkle with the spring onions and dill and serve immediately.

At MAZI, our hot plates are in the style of hot meze, designed to be shared by everyone around the table, as with our jars and salads, or served as part of a feast, such as the Feta Tempura (*see* page 140) and Zucchini Cakes (*see* page 138). They are, however, generally more substantial dishes and feature a different range of ingredients, and some of them can also be enjoyed on their own, such as *Gemista* (*see* page 115) and Artichokes à la Polita (*see* page 132). You will find a wide variety of recipes to choose from and a good mix of vegetarian, meat and seafood options.

We've drawn inspiration for these dishes from our childhood summers and holidays in Greece, and memories of our mothers' and grandmothers' cooking. Although many have been given the MAZI revamp, some are the classic recipes just as they have been handed down to us and how we prepare them at MAZI for our staff feasts.

HOT PLATES

CRISPY LAMB BELLY WITH MISO EGGPLANT AND CHICKPEA AND TAHINI PURÉE

We wanted to replicate the taste of the succulent, smoky grilled lamb cutlets to be enjoyed at a traditional village taverna in the Greek mountains. Lamb belly is a fatty, juicy piece of meat that serves well in recreating that authentic eating experience, and matching it with eggplant and a chickpea and tahini purée will leave you craving for more.

SERVES 4

olive oil
2 lamb breasts, cut into
    4 equal pieces
1 small onion, roughly chopped
1 carrot, peeled and roughly
    chopped
1 celery stick, roughly chopped
3 garlic cloves, halved
1 sprig of rosemary
5 eggplant
7 oz (200 ml) sunflower oil, for
    frying the eggplant
potato starch, for sprinkling
    over the eggplant
salt and pepper

for the miso paste
9 oz (250 ml) dry white wine
9 oz (250 g) superfine sugar
4 oz (120 ml) mirin
1 lb 2 oz (500 g) white miso
    paste (we use Hikari)

Preheat the oven to 350°F (180°C).

Heat a heavy-based frying pan over high heat until very hot and add a drizzle of olive oil. Season the lamb breasts with salt and pepper and sear them for 1–2 minutes on each side to get them a bit crispy and golden brown. Remove from the pan to a large oval casserole dish (ideally a cast-iron one, such as Le Creuset). Replace the oil in the frying pan with a fresh drizzle. Add the onion, carrot, celery and garlic and sweat over medium heat until softened. Transfer the vegetables to the casserole and add the rosemary. Pour over enough water to cover the lamb, cover with the lid and braise in the oven for 3 hours.

Meanwhile, prepare the miso paste. Set a smaller saucepan over a larger one containing some barely simmering water to create a double boiler. Add the wine, sugar and mirin, and stir until the sugar has dissolved. Add the miso paste and whisk until completely incorporated, then leave for about 2 hours until the mixture has reduced by half, stirring occasionally. Remove from the heat and set aside.

Peel the eggplant and cut them into big chunks. Put them in a colander, sprinkle with a very generous pinch of salt and set them aside to drain for an hour.

Remove the lamb belly from the oven and leave it to rest for an hour. While the lamb is resting, heat the sunflower oil in a deep saucepan over high heat. Pat the eggplant chunks dry with paper towels, then sprinkle with potato starch to coat. Fry in the hot oil, in batches, for 1 minute until crispy. Drain and place on a plate lined with paper towels to soak up the excess oil.

RECIPE CONTINUES...

for the chickpea and
tahini purée

1 lb 2 oz (500 g) soaked
    (*see* page 156) and cooked
    dried chickpeas (boiled
    for at least 50 minutes
    until soft) or use drained
    canned chickpeas
3½ oz (100 ml) water
juice of 1 lemon
1 tablespoon tahini
1 garlic clove, peeled
4 teaspoons extra-virgin
    olive oil
salt

to serve

pinch of sweet paprika
pinch of finely chopped
    cilantro leaves
sprinkling of nigella seeds

For the chickpea and tahini purée, blend all the ingredients together in a food processor or blender and set aside until ready to serve.

Towards the end of the lamb resting time, preheat the oven to 400°F (200°C). Heat a griddle pan over high heat, or an indoor grill if you have one — or use a barbecue in the summer months. Cut the lamb belly into thick strips and griddle or grill them on both sides until they are crispy on the outside. Meanwhile, brush the eggplant with the miso paste, place on a baking sheet and warm them up in the oven for a few minutes.

Serve the chickpea and tahini purée topped with the lamb belly strips and miso eggplant, sprinkled with the paprika, cilantro and nigella seeds.

for the filled cannelloni

5½ tablespoons (80 ml)
    extra-virgin olive oil
2 lb 4 oz (1 kg) ground beef
1 large white onion, chopped
2 garlic cloves, chopped
2 tablespoons dry white wine
7 oz (200 g) tomato purée
1 bay leaf
3–4 sprigs of thyme
3 cloves
1 cinnamon stick
pinch of sweet paprika
40 dried cannelloni
salt and pepper

for the tomato sauce

4 teaspoons extra-virgin
    olive oil
½ white onion, chopped
1 garlic clove, chopped
2 lb 4 oz (1 kg) tomatoes,
    deseeded and chopped
3½ oz (100 g) tomato purée
1 tablespoon superfine sugar
1 bay leaf
pinch of ground cinnamon
1 tablespoon salt
9 oz (250 ml) warm water

for the béchamel sauce

3½ oz (100 g) butter
3½ oz (100 g) all-purpose flour
4¼ cups (1 liter) milk
1 teaspoon sugar
pinch of ground nutmeg
pinch of salt
pinch of white pepper

SERVES 6

CANNELLONI PASTITSIO WITH GROUND BEEF AND BÉCHAMEL SAUCE

Our playful take on the traditional pasta and ground beef bake is very easy to make and also lighter on the stomach. If serving this dish as part of a feast, the recipe would make enough for 10 guests.

First make the tomato sauce. Heat the olive oil in a heavy-based saucepan, add the onion and garlic and sauté over medium heat until softened but not browned. Add the remaining ingredients for the sauce, cover and cook over low heat for 1½ hours.

Meanwhile, for the filled cannelloni, heat the olive oil in a separate pan, add the ground beef and sauté over medium heat, stirring and breaking up with a wooden spoon, until browned. Add the onion and garlic and sauté until softened but not browned. Pour in the wine and simmer briskly until it has completely evaporated. Add the remaining ingredients, except the cannelloni, and cook over low heat, uncovered, for about 20 minutes until the meat is tender and the mixture has thickened to a sauce consistency.

Preheat the oven to 400°F (200°C).

Cook the cannelloni in a large saucepan of salted boiling water according to the packet instructions until al dente. Drain well. Fill the cannelloni with the ground beef mixture. Spread the tomato sauce over the base of a baking dish, then place the filled cannelloni on top of the sauce.

For the béchamel sauce, melt the butter in a saucepan over medium heat, add the flour and cook, whisking with a balloon whisk, until a smooth paste (roux) forms. Gradually add the milk and cook until the mixture thickens, whisking constantly. Remove the pan from the heat and add the sugar, nutmeg, salt and white pepper. Pour the béchamel on top of the cannelloni and bake for 8–10 minutes until beginning to brown. Serve hot.

14 oz (400 g) boneless, rindless pork belly

3 teaspoons Dijon mustard

1 red onion, chopped

1 teaspoon sweet paprika, plus an extra sprinkling

1 teaspoon dried oregano, plus an extra sprinkling

4 rice paper wrappers

1 large tomato, quartered, deseeded and cut into fine strips

½ bunch of flat-leaf parsley, chopped

handful of nigella seeds

salt and pepper

fresh green salad, to serve (optional)

for the caramelized onions

2 tablespoons extra-virgin olive oil

1 red onion, finely sliced

¾ oz (20 g) superfine sugar

1–2 tablespoons red wine vinegar, to taste

for the mustard water

2 teaspoons Dijon mustard

2 garlic cloves, finely chopped

1 teaspoon dried oregano

10 oz (300 ml) cold water

for the garlic yogurt sauce

3½ oz (100 g) Greek yogurt

4 teaspoons extra-virgin olive oil

1 garlic clove, finely chopped

SERVES 4

COOL SOUVLAKI

Souvlaki is Greece's national street-food dish consisting of spit-roasted meat, wrapped in pita bread with *tzatziki* and onions, also called gyros. We have replaced the pitta with a rice paper wrapper and instead of the spit-roasted meat we roast a pork belly and then shred it to achieve a similar texture. The other traditional components of *souvlaki* are also given an Asian twist, resulting in what looks like a Vietnamese roll but with the flavor and feel of *souvlaki*. "Cool" refers to the coolness of the dish, not the temperature — hence the recipe's placement in our Hot Plates chapter.

Preheat the oven to 375°F (190°C).

Place the pork belly in a deep roasting pan. Smear over the mustard, then sprinkle with the onion, paprika and oregano and add a good grinding of pepper. Pour in enough water so that the pork is completely submerged. Cover with parchment paper and then foil and cook for about 4 hours. Remove from the oven and leave to cool.

Meanwhile, prepare the accompaniments. For the caramelized onions, heat the oil in a frying pan, add the onion and cook over medium heat until soft. Add the sugar and vinegar and cook until the onions are caramelized. For the mustard water, mix all the ingredients together thoroughly in a bowl large enough for dunking your wrappers. For the garlic yogurt sauce, mix all the ingredients together in a separate bowl and season with salt and pepper.

Cut the cooled pork into strips. Heat a large, heavy-based frying pan or griddle pan over medium-high heat. Add the pork strips and cook for just a minute or two on each side until hot and crispy. Remove from the pan and add the extra sprinkling of paprika and oregano.

To assemble the *souvlaki* wraps, soak 2 wrappers in the mustard water until soft. Remove from the water and lay them flat on a cutting board. Divide half the tomato strips, caramelized onion, pork and parsley between the wrappers, placing the ingredients in the middle of each, then sprinkle with nigella seeds and grind over a good amount of salt and pepper. Repeat with the remaining 2 wrappers.

Starting from the edge nearest to you, roll each wrapper up, tucking in the sides as you go so that the filling is completely enclosed. Leave to dry for 5 minutes, then cut each roll in half. Serve your wraps at room temperature or turn once or twice in a hot frying pan to warm. Accompany with the garlic yogurt sauce, and a fresh green salad, if liked.

1 lb 2 oz (500 g) ground pork
1 lb 2 oz (500 g) ground beef
3½ oz (100 g) panko
    breadcrumbs
3 garlic cloves, chopped
1 white onion, chopped
1 bunch of flat-leaf parsley,
    chopped, plus extra
    to garnish
1 tablespoon ground
    cinnamon
1 teaspoon ground cumin
1 egg, beaten
5 oz (150 ml) extra-virgin olive
    oil, plus extra for shallow-
    frying
all-purpose flour, for sprinkling
salt and pepper
steamed basmati rice,
    to serve

for the tomato sauce
3 tablespoons extra-virgin
    olive oil
1 small onion, chopped
3 garlic cloves, chopped
7 oz (200 g) tomato purée
18 oz (500 ml) water
3 sprigs of thyme
1 bay leaf
1 heaped tablespoon sugar
2 pinches of ground cumin
1 pinch of sweet paprika
salt and pepper

SERVES 6–8

SOUTZOUKAKIA FROM SMYRNA

At the restaurant, we serve this traditional dish of baked meatballs in tomato sauce as a jar, but since it's so delicious, we felt we had to move it center stage and include it in this section of the book. Full of flavor with a distinctive Anatolian air, the recipe originates from the Greeks of Smyrna (modern-day Izmir, Turkey), and after being introduced to Greek cuisine in the early 20th century it became a Sunday lunch sensation. Serve this with buttery or steamed basmati rice as a more substantial dish, or on its own as a meze.

Put the ground meats with all the remaining main ingredients, except the flour, in a large bowl, then mix well and knead the mixture together with your hands. Shape the mixture into about 30–40 fat cigar-like sausages, cover and chill in the refrigerator for an hour.

Meanwhile, prepare the tomato sauce. Heat the oil in a deep saucepan, add the onion and garlic and sauté over medium heat until soft but not browned. Add the tomato purée and cook, stirring, for about 1 minute. Add the measured water and the remaining ingredients and cook until the mixture has thickened. Remove the thyme sprigs and bay leaf, then transfer the mixture to a food processor or blender and blend until smooth. Return the sauce to the pan.

Heat enough oil for shallow-frying in a large frying pan over medium heat. Sprinkle the *soutzoukakia* with flour, add to the hot oil and fry, turning frequently, for about 5 minutes until cooked through.

For a lighter dish, you can bake them in the oven instead. Preheat the oven to 425°F (220°C). Brush a baking sheet with olive oil, add the *soutzoukakia* and bake for 10 minutes, turning frequently, until browned.

Return the tomato sauce to the heat and add the *soutzoukakia*. Simmer for 4–5 minutes so that the *soutzoukakia* absorb the flavors of the sauce.

Sprinkle with chopped parsley and serve with steamed basmati rice.

2 rabbits, jointed (ask your
    butcher to do this for you)
3 garlic cloves, peeled but
    left whole
3 bay leaves
2 sprigs of rosemary
½ bunch of thyme
10 black peppercorns
8½ cups (2 liters) red wine
9 oz (250 ml) red wine vinegar
extra-virgin olive oil
1 large white onion, roughly
    chopped
2 carrots, peeled and roughly
    chopped
2 celery sticks, roughly
    chopped
7 oz (200 g) tomato purée
14 oz (400 g) can good-quality
    chopped tomatoes
5 cloves
5 allspice berries
18 oz (500 ml) vegetable stock
2 lb 4 oz (1 kg) pearl (baby or
    silverskin) onions, peeled
    but left whole
salt and pepper
microgreens, to garnish

SERVES 8

Mouthwateringly tender,
this is one of the few game
dishes to feature in Greek
cuisine. It is a big casserole
dish that slow-cooks for
hours with shallots, red
wine and lots of spices;
here we've used pearl
(baby) onions instead.
You can replace the rabbit
in this fantastic winter
warmer with the same
amount of beef or veal.

SHREDDED RABBIT STIFADO

Season the rabbit pieces with salt and pepper, then add to a large glass or ceramic bowl with the garlic cloves, bay leaves, rosemary, thyme, black peppercorns, wine and vinegar. Cover and leave the rabbit to marinate in the refrigerator for 8 hours or overnight.

Remove the rabbit pieces from the marinade and pat dry with paper towels. Strain the marinade to remove the herbs and spices, then reserve 3 cups (700 ml) of the liquid.

Heat a large saucepan over medium-high heat and add a drizzle of extra-virgin olive oil. Brown the rabbit pieces, in batches, on both sides, transferring from the pan to a large roasting pan (or a lidded casserole dish). Add the white onion, carrots and celery to the pan and sauté over medium heat until softened. Add the tomato purée and chopped tomatoes, cloves and allspice, then pour in the reserved marinade. Stir well and simmer briskly until reduced by half, then stir in the stock. Meanwhile, preheat the oven to 350°F (180°C).

Pour the vegetable mixture over the rabbit in the roasting pan (or casserole dish). Cover with foil (or the lid) and bake in the oven for 1½ hours until cooked through. Remove from the oven and leave to cool.

Lift the rabbit pieces out of the sauce, then remove the meat from the bone and shred it. Set aside in a bowl. Pass the sauce through a strainer into a saucepan. Bring to a boil and cook until reduced. Add the whole pearl onions and cook for a further 10 minutes or until the onions are soft and the sauce is thick. Finally, add the shredded rabbit meat to the sauce and heat through before serving garnished with microgreens.

THE SAUCE
CRIES OUT FOR
SOME HOMEMADE
FRIES FOR DIPPING
(*SEE PAGE 157*).

LAMB SHOULDER BAKLAVAS WITH CUMIN YOGURT

Perfect for sharing, you can serve these lamb-filled filo pastry rolls as canapés or meze for a dinner party. In the early days of MAZI, we featured them as one element of a larger lamb dish. Having proved to be undoubtedly the favorite part of the dish, we decided to turn the baklavas into a main event.

4 lb 8 oz (2 kg) shoulder of lamb on the bone
10 garlic cloves, peeled
3½ oz (100 g) Dijon mustard
½ bunch of thyme
1 carrot, peeled and roughly chopped
1 onion, roughly chopped
2 celery sticks, roughly chopped
6⅓ cups (1.5 liters) water
3½ oz (100 ml) olive oil, plus extra for brushing
2 bunches of spring onions, chopped
2 bunches of flat-leaf parsley, chopped
3 sheets of filo pastry
salt and pepper

for the cumin yogurt
1 lb 2 oz (500 g) Greek yogurt
3½ oz (100 ml) extra-virgin olive oil
grated zest of 1 lemon
juice of 1 lime
1 tablespoon ground cumin
pinch of salt
pinch of pepper

SERVES 8–10

Preheat the oven to 400°F (200°C).

Season the lamb shoulder with salt and pepper. Using the tip of a sharp knife, make 10 evenly spaced incisions in the meat and insert a garlic clove into each incision. Rub the lamb with the mustard, then place in a roasting pan and throw in the thyme, carrot, onion and celery. Add the measured water (it should come three-quarters of the way up the lamb shoulder) and cover with foil. Bake for 4 hours until the meat is falling off the bone, turning the meat on to its other side halfway through. Remove the pan from the oven and leave the lamb to rest for 30 minutes.

Lift the meat out of the pan and shred with your hands or 2 forks.

Mix the meat with the olive oil, spring onions and parsley in a large bowl. Season well with salt and pepper.

Preheat the oven to 475°F (240°C). Line a baking sheet with parchment paper.

Lay a sheet of filo pastry horizontally on a work surface and place one-third of the lamb mixture in a row about 1½ inches (4 cm) wide across the sheet about the same distance from the edge of the pastry sheet nearest to you. Lift up and fold the pastry edge over the filling, then roll up in the sheet of filo into a cylinder. Cut the cylinder into lengths of about 2¾ inches (7 cm). Repeat with the remaining lamb mixture and filo pastry sheets.

Place the rolls on the lined baking sheet, brush them with olive oil and bake for 8 minutes until golden.

Meanwhile, mix the ingredients for the cumin yogurt together in a bowl until well combined.

Serve the baklavas warm with the cumin yogurt for dipping on the side.

GEMISTA

This colorful dish of stuffed vegetables is the MAZI team's favorite summer dish. We have devised many different versions for our menu over the years, including an "inside-out" risotto-style interpretation (see page 56). This is the original recipe using ground beef. We advise you to reserve this dish for cooking during the summer when the vegetables are at their best, and if you make it a day in advance, it will taste even better. Add a slice of feta and it's unbeatable!

3 eggplant
5 small green peppers
2 small red peppers or Romano peppers
2 beef tomatoes
2 potatoes, peeled and quartered

for the filling

4–5 tablespoons extra-virgin olive oil, to taste
2 large onions, finely chopped
4 garlic cloves, finely chopped
1 lb 5 oz (600 g) ground beef
7 oz (200 ml) red wine
2 × 14 oz (400 g) cans good-quality chopped tomatoes
1 teaspoon tomato purée
pinch of sugar
1¾ oz (50 g) flat-leaf parsley, finely chopped
5 tablespoons short-grain rice
salt and pepper

for the sauce

2 × 14 oz (400 g) cans good-quality chopped tomatoes
5 tablespoons (75 ml) extra-virgin olive oil
salt and pepper

SERVES 6

Arrange the eggplant, peppers and tomatoes standing upright in a roasting pan so that they fit together. Add the potatoes to fill the gaps in between the other vegetables.

For the filling, heat the the oil in a large sauté pan over high heat, add the onions and garlic and sauté for about 3 minutes until softened but not browned. Add the ground beef and cook, stirring and breaking up with a wooden spoon, until well browned and it starts sticking to the base of the pan. Season with salt and pepper, then add the red wine and continue cooking until the wine has evaporated. Add the chopped tomatoes, tomato purée, sugar and finally the parsley. Reduce the heat and cook for a further 20–30 minutes. Remove the pan from the heat, add the rice and mix well.

While the filling is cooking, cut the top off each of the eggplant, peppers and tomatoes, reserving the lids, and scoop out the insides. Discard the core and seeds of the peppers, but reserve the eggplant flesh for another dish (sauté with garlic and parsley, add some tomato sauce and serve with pasta, or use in a risotto). Place the tomato flesh in a large bowl.

Preheat the oven to 400°F (200°C).

Using a tablespoon, fill the vegetable cavities with the ground beef mixture. Return each vegetable to its original position in the roasting pan and then replace their lids.

For the sauce, add the canned chopped tomatoes to the fresh tomato flesh in the bowl along with the olive oil and a good seasoning of salt and pepper. Mix well and then pour in between the stuffed vegetables, covering any gaps, but not on top of the vegetables.

Bake for 1½–2 hours until the vegetables are soft, turning them around every 20 minutes so that they cook evenly without burning on one side. Depending on the strength of your oven, they may be ready a little sooner — the key is to keep an eye on how the vegetables are doing and turn them regularly. Serve once the vegetables are done.

Tzatziki (*see* page 51),
    to serve
tomatoes, cut into thin wedges,
    to garnish (optional)

for the meatballs

2 lb 4 oz (1 kg) ground beef
1 white onion, finely chopped
6 tablespoons (90 ml) extra-
    virgin olive oil
3 tablespoons red wine vinegar
3 garlic cloves, finely chopped
3¼ oz (90 g) panko
    breadcrumbs
1 bunch of mint, chopped
1 bunch of flat-leaf parsley,
    chopped
4 teaspoons salt
2 pinches of pepper
1 egg, beaten
drizzle of olive oil

for the handmade chips

1 large fluffy-textured potato,
    such as russet
sunflower oil, for deep-frying
pinch of salt
pinch of dried oregano

**SERVES 8; MAKES
40 MEATBALLS**

Filled with childhood
memories, this recipe
has been adored by
our customers through
the years. These MAZI
meatballs are light, fluffy
and wonderfully aromatic,
and pair perfectly with
tzatziki. Served with hand-
crafted chips, this dish
appeals just as much to
kids as grown-ups.

GRANDMAMA'S MEATBALLS WITH HANDMADE CHIPS

Put all the ingredients for the meatballs, except the olive oil, in a large bowl and mix them together well with your hands. Cover and leave to rest in the refrigerator for an hour.

Meanwhile, for the handmade chips, peel the potato and then cut into thin slices with a vegetable peeler. Rinse the potato slices in cold water until the water runs clear, then drain thoroughly and pat dry.

Heat enough sunflower oil for deep-frying in a deep-fryer or a large, deep saucepan to 400°F (200°C). Deep-fry the potato slices in the hot oil, in batches, for about 1 minute until golden. Remove carefully with a slotted spoon, drain and place on a plate lined with paper towels to soak up the excess oil. Sprinkle with the salt and oregano.

Preheat the oven to 400°F (200°C). Roll the meatball mixture into small balls of 1–1¼ oz (30–35 g) each. Place the meatballs on a baking sheet, drizzle with olive oil and bake for 8–10 minutes. Remove from the oven and leave them to rest for a few minutes.

Reheat the sunflower oil for deep-frying to 375–400°F (190–200°C). Deep-fry the meatballs in the hot oil, in batches, for about 1 minute until crispy on the outside. Remove carefully with a slotted spoon, drain and place on a plate lined with paper towels to soak up the excess oil, then serve hot with the chips and *tzatziki*, and the tomato garnish, if liked.

extra-virgin olive oil
1 shallot, finely chopped
1 garlic clove, finely chopped
7 oz (200 g) Calasparra rice
dry white wine
18 oz (500 ml) vegetable stock,
    plus extra if needed
6 uncooked king prawns,
    heads removed, peeled and
    deveined, then cut into thick
    pieces
1 baby squid (calamari),
    cleaned and head/tentacles
    separated, diced
16 live clams
2 pinches of saffron threads
1 bunch of flat-leaf parsley,
    chopped
juice of 1½ lemons
½ oz (15 g) butter
¾ oz (20 g) Parmesan cheese,
    grated
1 bunch of chives, chopped

for the roasted tomato sauce
20 cherry tomatoes, halved
pinch of sugar
2 garlic cloves, halved
3 sprigs of thyme
drizzle of extra-virgin olive oil
salt and pepper

SERVES 4

This rice-based dish is full
of vibrant colors and flavors.
Do use Calasparra paella
rice (try Spanish food stores
or online suppliers) for the
best result, as it's highly
absorbent and prevents the
dish from turning sticky.
If clams are not available,
mussels work well here too.

CLAM AND PRAWN PILAFI WITH ROASTED TOMATOES, LEMON AND SAFFRON

First make the roasted tomato sauce. Preheat the oven to 400°F (200°C). Spread the cherry tomatoes out on a baking sheet. Sprinkle with the sugar, some salt and pepper, the halved garlic cloves, thyme sprigs and olive oil and roast for 15–20 minutes.

Remove from the oven and discard the thyme sprigs. Transfer the roasted tomatoes to a food processor or blender and blend until smooth.

Heat a drizzle of olive oil in a deep saucepan, add three-quarters of the shallot and sweat over medium heat until soft. Add three-quarters of the garlic, then stir in the rice and cook for about 1 minute. Add a drizzle of white wine and cook until it has evaporated. Pour in the vegetable stock and cook for 15–20 minutes until the rice is al dente, adding more stock if needed. Stir in the prawns and calamari and cook for a few minutes until the prawns turn pink and the calamari opaque, then add 3–4 tablespoons of the tomato sauce.

Meanwhile, wash the clams well in cold water (don't use any that are open and won't close when sharply tapped). Heat a drizzle of olive oil in a separate saucepan, add the clams, cover with the lid and cook for 3–5 minutes until the clams start opening (discard any that don't open). Add the remaining shallot and garlic, another drizzle of white wine and a pinch of saffron and cook until the wine has reduced. Then fold in a pinch of the chopped parsley and half the lemon juice.

Remove the rice from the heat and add the remaining pinch of saffron, the butter and Parmesan. Finish with the remaining chopped parsley, the chives and the rest of the lemon juice. Mix to combine, then transfer to a serving bowl and place the clams on top to serve.

SEARED SCALLOPS WITH BLACK QUINOA AND BABY BEETS

This simple, light, healthy and delicious dish is good all year round, although we like to serve it at MAZI during the summer months. Black quinoa has a more pronounced flavor and crunchier texture than regular white quinoa and is especially prized by chefs.

6 raw baby beets
  (or 12 if very small)
extra-virgin olive oil
drizzle of red wine vinegar
10½ oz (300 g) black quinoa
10 green beans, sliced into thin
  rounds
4 spring onions, chopped
handful of dill, chopped
handful of flat-leaf parsley,
  chopped
handful of chives, chopped
½ quantity of Vinaigrette
  (see page 82)
12 shelled uncooked king
  scallops
salt and white pepper
microgreens, to garnish
  (optional)

SERVES 4

Put the beets in a saucepan and cover with cold water, then add a drizzle of the olive oil and the red wine vinegar. Bring to a boil and then cook over medium heat for 15–20 minutes, depending on their size, until they are soft. Drain them and leave to cool. Peel off the skins, then cut the beets into quarters and set aside.

Rinse the quinoa, then put in a saucepan, cover well with water and bring to a boil. Cook for 10–15 minutes until soft, then drain and leave to cool.

Mix the cooled quinoa with the raw beans, spring onions and all the chopped herbs in a bowl. Season to taste with salt, then add the vinaigrette and gently mix with the salad ingredients.

Heat a heavy-based frying pan until smoking hot, add a drizzle of olive oil and sear the scallops for about 1–2 minutes on each side until golden and crisp yet still tender in the center. Sprinkle with white pepper and remove from the pan.

Place the beets and scallops on top of the quinoa salad and serve garnished with microgreens, if liked.

2 lb 4 oz (1 kg) tomatoes, halved

14 oz (400 g) can good-quality
chopped tomatoes

1 red chili, roughly chopped

½ small white onion, peeled

3 garlic cloves, peeled

1 tablespoon extra-virgin
olive oil

1 tablespoon superfine sugar

1 shot of ouzo (2 if you want
a more powerful flavor)

sunflower oil, for deep-frying

24 uncooked king prawns,
heads removed, peeled and
deveined

9 oz (250 g) feta cheese,
crumbled

10½ oz (300 g) Metsovone
cheese (see page 42) or any
yellow smoked hard cheese,
crumbled

salt and pepper

for the tempura batter

14 oz (400 g) store-bought
tempura batter mix

20 oz (600 ml) cold water

to serve

1¾ oz (50 g) feta cheese

sprinkling of chopped
flat-leaf parsley

SERVES 6

KING PRAWN SAGANAKI WITH OUZO AND METSOVONE

Saganaki is also the name of the small frying pan that this dish is habitually cooked in, a wonderful blend of cooked prawns, tomatoes, ouzo, melt-in-the-mouth feta and smoky Metsovone. It's a perfect dish for any season of the year. Our twist on the traditional recipe is that instead of cooking the prawns in the sauce, we deep-fry them tempura style and place them on top.

Wrap the 1¾ oz (50 g) feta to serve in plastic wrap and place in the freezer.

Put the fresh tomatoes, canned tomatoes, chili, onion, garlic, olive oil and sugar in a food processor or blender and blend very thoroughly, then pass through a fine-mesh strainer into a saucepan. Boil the mixture for 20 minutes until reduced and thick. Season to taste with salt, remove from the heat and pour in the ouzo. Transfer the mixture to an oval terracotta or ceramic baking dish. Preheat the oven to 400°F (200°C).

Whisk the tempura batter mix with the measured water in a bowl, then cover and leave to rest in the refrigerator for at least 10 minutes.

Heat enough sunflower oil for deep-frying in a deep-fryer or a large, deep saucepan to 340°F (170°C). Season the prawns with salt and pepper, dip them into the tempura batter and deep-fry in the hot oil, in batches, for 1–2 minutes until golden. Drain and place on a plate lined with paper towels to soak up the excess oil.

While you are frying the prawns, sprinkle the crumbled cheeses over the tomato sauce in the baking dish and bake in the oven for 5–6 minutes.

Remove the dish from the oven and place the prawns on top, then sprinkle with chopped parsley. Finally, take the feta out of the freezer and finely grate it directly on to the prawns before serving.

LIGHTLY BATTERED ROCK OYSTERS

Fried mussels are a typical Greek delicacy, served with a good squeeze of lemon juice. Inspired by that classic, we created this dish using fried oysters instead. This recipe will make more herb oil than you will need for the oysters. You can store the remainder in the refrigerator for up to 2 weeks.

12 live rock oysters
8½ oz (240 ml) extra-virgin olive oil
1 red chili, very finely chopped
1 garlic clove, crushed
½ bunch of chives, finely chopped
½ bunch of cilantro, finely chopped
grated zest of 1 lime
grated zest and juice of 1 lemon, plus extra juice to serve (optional)
sunflower oil, for deep-frying

for the tempura batter
7 oz (200 g) store-bought tempura batter mix
10 oz (300 ml) cold water

MAKES 12

Whisk the tempura batter mix with the measured water in a bowl, then cover and leave to rest in the refrigerator while you prepare the oysters, or for at least 10 minutes.

Follow the method on page 79 to clean and shuck the oysters, removing and reserving the oyster meat, then washing and drying the bottom shells.

Mix the olive oil with the chili, garlic, herbs and lime and lemon zest.

Heat enough sunflower oil for deep-frying in a deep-fryer or a large, deep saucepan to 375°F (190°C). Dip the oysters into the tempura batter and deep-fry in the hot oil, in batches, for about 1 minute until golden brown. Drain and place on a plate lined with paper towels to soak up the excess oil, then squeeze over the lemon juice.

Place the deep-fried oysters back in their shells and pour a teaspoon of the herb oil on top of each one. You can then squeeze a little more lemon juice over the oysters if you like before serving.

WARM CHERRY TOMATOES WITH GOAT CHEESE AND THYME OIL

This recipe is guaranteed to transport you to the Aegean, the fragrant thyme and piquant capers in combination with the honey-glazed tomatoes and goat cheese giving you the quintessential taste of a Greek holiday. The secret to its success is the large quantity of fresh thyme used to make the flavored oil, which you can buy in bulk online or from some specialty produce markets. Make sure you serve the dish with plenty of bread to dip into the oil.

10 cherry tomatoes
7 oz (200 g) thyme leaves
14 oz (400 ml) extra-virgin
    olive oil
good pinch of salt
¾ oz (20 g) honey
¼ oz (10 g) butter, diced
4½ oz (130 g) soft goat cheese
handful of capers

SERVES 4

Blanch the tomatoes in boiling water for 20–30 seconds, then transfer to a bowl of ice-cold water to cool quickly. Drain them and then peel them and pat them dry.

Blend the thyme leaves with the olive oil and salt in a food processor or blender until well combined, then set aside.

Put the tomatoes in a saucepan, add the honey and warm over a gentle heat, stirring gently to glaze them. Once the honey thickens, add the butter and move the pan around to mix it in as it melts.

Roll the goat cheese into small balls, a little smaller than a golf ball, place on a baking sheet and warm them up under a preheated hot grill for 1 minute. Transfer them to a serving plate.

Add the glazed tomatoes to the goat cheese, scatter over the capers and pour the thyme oil around the ingredients, then serve immediately.

ARTICHOKES À LA POLITA

Many people may not be aware of this, but Greek cuisine is one of the few around the world that has a plethora of vegetarian and vegan dishes. We call this treatment of artichokes à la Polita because the dish originates from "Poli," aka Constantinople, now Istanbul. At the restaurant we serve artichoke hearts with monkfish, scallops and mussels in an egg and lemon sauce, but the recipe is too fiddly to recreate at home, so we decided to feature the original, which is just as delicious, as well as being healthy and vegan.

8 fresh globe artichokes,
    or frozen artichoke
    hearts, defrosted
1 lemon, halved (if preparing
    fresh artichokes)
7¾ oz (220 ml) extra-virgin
    olive oil
1 onion, grated or finely
    chopped
1 bunch of spring onions,
    chopped
2 large carrots, peeled and
    cut into rounds
3 large potatoes, peeled and
    quartered
1 bunch of dill, finely chopped
3½ oz (100 g) fresh peas
9 oz (250 ml) hot water
salt and pepper

SERVES 4

If using fresh artichokes, to prepare them, rinse them well, then trim the end of the stem. Peel away all the petals (these are not used for this dish) until you reach the heart, then scoop out the hairy choke from the base with a teaspoon. Peel the stem with a vegetable peeler. Rub with the cut side of the lemon halves to prevent discoloration.

You will need a wide, shallow pan with a lid. Heat the olive oil in the pan over medium-high heat, add the onion and spring onions and sauté until softened but not browned. Add the carrots and sauté until softened.

Add the artichoke hearts and all the remaining ingredients to the pan with a good seasoning of salt and pepper. Cover with the lid and cook over low heat for 30 minutes or until the potatoes and artichokes are soft (you may need to add a little more water), then serve when ready.

IMAM BAYILDI EGGPLANT WITH STILTON

Many folk stories and myths surround the origin of imam bayildi, literally meaning "the imam fainted," which dates back to the era when Greece was under the rule of the Ottoman Empire. It traditionally consists of eggplant, tomatoes, onions and garlic, but drawing on our local influences in London, we have introduced the classic English Stilton cheese to give it an unusual twist.

7 oz (200 g) tomatoes

drizzle of extra-virgin olive oil

1 lb 5 oz (600 g) white onions, sliced

3 garlic cloves, chopped

3½ oz (100 g) tomato purée

3 tablespoons superfine sugar

1½ oz (40 g) flat-leaf parsley, chopped, plus a few shredded leaves to serve

1 cinnamon stick

2 bay leaves

9 oz (250 ml) water

sunflower oil, for shallow-frying

3 eggplant, halved lengthways

4 teaspoons hoisin sauce

14 oz (400 g) Stilton cheese, crumbled

salt and pepper

SERVES 6

Add the tomatoes to a food processor or blender and blend to a purée.

Heat the olive oil in a deep saucepan, add the onions and sweat over medium heat until soft. Add the garlic and sauté until soft but not browned, then stir in the tomato purée, sugar and puréed tomatoes. Season to taste with salt and pepper and add the chopped parsley, cinnamon stick and bay leaves. Pour in the measured water and simmer, uncovered, until the liquid has reduced and the mixture is a thick sauce consistency. Set aside.

Preheat the oven to 400°F (200°C).

Heat a shallow depth of sunflower oil in a large frying pan, add the eggplant halves and fry over medium heat for about 6 minutes until softened, turning occasionally. Drain and place on a plate lined with paper towels to soak up the excess oil.

Brush the eggplant with the hoisin sauce and place, cut side up, in a baking dish in a single layer. Top with the sauce so that the eggplant are completely covered. Scatter over the Stilton and bake for 15–20 minutes until the cheese has just melted.

Serve hot, sprinkled with shredded parsley leaves.

1 lb 9 oz (700 g) zucchini

1 large russet potato

7 oz (200 g) Metsovone cheese, grated

7 oz (200 g) feta cheese, crumbled

1 bunch of spring onions, chopped

handful of mint leaves, chopped

½ bunch of dill, chopped

3½ oz (100 g) panko breadcrumbs

1 tablespoon black sesame seeds

2 eggs, beaten

sunflower oil, for deep-frying

salt and pepper

for the coating

3 egg whites

10½ oz (300 g) panko breadcrumbs

for the cucumber and mint dip

1 lb 2 oz (500 g) superfine sugar

5 oz (150 ml) white rice vinegar

1½ tablespoons mirin

1 Scotch bonnet chili

1 large cucumber, peeled and left whole, skin reserved and finely diced

a few mint leaves, plus extra to garnish

1½ small red chilies, finely diced

SERVES 8; MAKES 24 CAKES

ZUCCHINI CAKES WITH CUCUMBER AND MINT DIP

Broadly known as kolokithokeftedes, these zucchini fritters are a great vegetarian alternative to meatballs, usually enjoyed with some tzatziki (see page 51) or Greek yogurt on the side. In our version, we coat the cakes with Japanese panko breadcrumbs to make them super crispy on the outside while keeping them juicy on the inside. The accompanying cucumber and mint dip is cooling and refreshing, but also includes an infusion of Scotch bonnet chili to give the dish an extra buzz.

If you can't find Metsovone cheese (see page 42), you can use Provolone or smoked Cheddar.

Grate the zucchini into a strainer, sprinkle with a very generous pinch of salt and leave them to drain for about an hour. Squeeze all the liquid out with your hands.

Meanwhile, peel the potato and cut into small pieces. Cook in a saucepan of boiling water until soft. Drain well and leave to cool.

Add the cooled potato to a large bowl with all the remaining ingredients (apart from the oil for frying), adding the grated zucchini at the end, and mix with your hands thoroughly. Shape the mixture into small cakes about 1–1¼ oz (30–35 g) each and set aside.

For the dip, add the sugar, vinegar and mirin to a saucepan and heat gently, stirring, until the sugar has dissolved. Transfer to a bowl, add the whole Scotch bonnet, peeled whole cucumber and mint and leave to cool and infuse. Once cooled, remove the Scotch bonnet, cucumber and mint and replace with the finely diced cucumber skin and chilies. Sprinkle a few mint leaves on top.

Heat enough sunflower oil for deep-frying in a deep-fryer or a large, deep saucepan to 375°F (190°C). Whisk the egg whites with a hint of water in a shallow bowl. Put the breadcrumbs in a separate shallow bowl. Roll the cakes first in the egg whites and then in the breadcrumbs. Deep-fry the cakes in the hot oil, in batches, for 2–3 minutes until golden brown.

Drain and place on a plate lined with paper towels to soak up the excess oil. Serve the zucchini cakes hot with the dip.

sunflower oil, for deep-frying
1 lb 2 oz (500 g) feta cheese,
    cut into 10 pieces
rosemary sprigs and
    microgreens, to garnish

for the lemon marmalade
1¾ oz (50 g) superfine sugar
4 oz (125 ml) freshly
    squeezed lemon juice
    (from about 2½ lemons)
pinch of saffron threads
    (optional)
13 oz (375 ml) water
scant ¼ oz (9 g) agar agar
    powder

for the caper meringue
9 oz (250 g) superfine sugar
5 tablespoons (75 ml) water
3 egg whites
1 teaspoon capers, finely
    chopped

for the tempura batter
8 oz (225 g) all-purpose flour
8 oz (225 g) corn meal
1 tablespoon baking powder
18 oz (500 ml) milk
sprinkling of black sesame
    seeds

SERVES 5

A famous London food
critic once wrote about this
dish: "It sounds absolutely
bonkers, but tastes heavenly
and it has been beautifully
crafted by a master." Try it
and judge for yourself!

FETA TEMPURA WITH CAPER MERINGUE AND LEMON MARMALADE

First make the lemon marmalade. Put the sugar, lemon juice, saffron, if using, and measured water in a saucepan and bring to a boil, stirring until the sugar has dissolved. Stir in the agar agar and continue to boil, stirring, for another minute until the agar agar has completely dissolved. Remove from the heat and pour into a heatproof bowl. Leave to cool and set. Once cooled, pour into a food processor or blender and blend until the mixture is completely smooth.

For the caper meringue, put the sugar and measured water in a saucepan and bring to a boil, stirring until the sugar has dissolved. Add a sugar thermometer to the pan and continue to boil until the syrup reaches 250°F (120°C).

Put the egg whites in the bowl of a stand mixer fitted with the whisk attachment and whisk on high speed until they start foaming. While the mixer is running, add the hot syrup in a slow, steady stream. Continue to whisk until the meringue mixture has cooled to room temperature, then fold in the finely chopped capers. Cover and chill in the refrigerator for about 30 minutes until set.

For the tempura batter, whisk all the ingredients, except the sesame seeds, together using the cleaned stand mixer. Then add the sesame seeds and stir in by hand. Cover and leave to rest in the refrigerator for at least 10 minutes.

Heat enough sunflower oil for deep-frying in a deep-fryer or a large, deep saucepan to 375°F (190°C). Dip the feta pieces in the tempura batter until well coated, then deep-fry in the hot oil, in batches, for 2–3 minutes until golden brown. Drain and place on a plate lined with paper towels to soak up the excess oil.

Pipe some caper meringue on top of each piece of feta and brown it with a blow torch for 2 seconds. Add a teaspoon of lemon marmalade alongside. Alternatively, serve the caper meringue and lemon marmalade on the side, but make sure that each mouthful combines all the components. Serve on a bed of rosemary and garnish with microgreens.

ZUCCHINI FLOWERS STUFFED WITH GOAT CHEESE

A delicacy of the summer months, zucchini flowers are usually stuffed with rice or fresh myzithra cheese (see page 170) in Greek cuisine. We use a soft goat cheese instead and the result is gorgeous! Serve these as a meze with other small dishes and/or salads. We like to serve these with red pepper coulis in the restaurant but they taste just as good without.

14 oz (400 g) soft goat cheese, crumbled and at room temperature
12 zucchini flowers with baby zucchini attached
sunflower oil, for deep-frying
salt

for the tempura batter
7 oz (200 g) store-bought tempura batter mix
10 oz (300 ml) cold water
pinch of salt
pinch of pepper

SERVES 4

For the tempura batter, whisk all the ingredients together in a bowl, then cover and leave to rest in the refrigerator for at least 10 minutes.

Meanwhile, fill a piping bag with the goat cheese. Open the zucchini flowers very carefully without breaking them or separating them from the zucchini, then carefully pipe in the goat cheese. Close the flowers gently, being careful not to make any holes.

Heat enough sunflower oil for deep-frying in a deep-fryer or a large, deep saucepan to 375°F (190°C). Dip the zucchini flowers only into the tempura batter, still attached to the zucchini, and deep-fry in the hot oil, in batches, for 1–2 minutes until golden brown. Drain and place on a plate lined with paper towels to soak up the excess oil. Arrange 3 zucchini flowers on each plate. Sprinkle the zucchini only with salt, then serve immediately.

SCRAMBLED EGGS STRAPATSADA

Don't be misled by the title of this recipe — scrambled eggs can be enjoyed any time of day, not just for breakfast. Strapatsada, to use its Greek name, is undeniably a summertime dish when tomatoes are at their best. Pair it with a Greek Salad (see page 74) and some homemade fries (see page 157) to make the perfect lunch or dinner.

6 tablespoons (90 ml) extra-
    virgin olive oil
1 long green pepper, or
    1 green chili if you prefer
    it spicy hot (or both!),
    deseeded and sliced into
    very thin rounds
10 large ripe tomatoes, grated
generous pinch of sugar
8 eggs
3½ oz (100 g) feta cheese,
    crumbled
pinch of dried oregano
    (optional)
salt and pepper

to serve
Greek Salad (see page 74)
Perfect Fries (see page 157)

SERVES 4–5

Heat the olive oil in a deep saucepan, add the green pepper or chili and sauté over medium heat until softened. Add the tomatoes, sugar and salt to taste and continue cooking over medium heat until all the tomato juices have evaporated and the mixture has thickened to a sauce consistency.

Reduce the heat and crack the eggs into the pan, one at a time, whisking constantly and mixing them with the sauce until just cooked. Add the crumbled feta, and the oregano if you wish, then remove the pan from the heat. Be careful not to overcook the eggs, bearing in mind that they will continue cooking off the heat with the heat of the pan and the sauce. Grind over some pepper and serve immediately accompanied by Greek Salad and Perfect Fries.

6 eggs
9 oz (250 ml) milk
9 oz (250 g) all-purpose flour
10½ oz (300 g) Metsovone
    cheese, grated
14 oz (400 g) talagani cheese,
    grated
9 oz (250 g) feta cheese,
    crumbled
sunflower oil, for deep-frying
5 egg whites
14 oz (400 g) panko
    breadcrumbs
salt and pepper

for the tomato jam
1 lb 2 oz (500 g) tomatoes
2 tablespoons olive oil
1¼ oz (35 g) white onion,
    finely chopped
½ garlic clove, chopped
6¼ oz (180 g) superfine sugar
2 cloves
juice of ½ lemon
1 teaspoon tomato purée
5 basil leaves
salt and pepper

SERVES 8–10

We took the traditional
concept of cheese saganaki,
which consists of melted
cheese with tomatoes
cooked and served in a little
pan of the same name, and
came up with these delicious
mini croquettes.

If you can't find Metsovone
(see page 42), use smoked
Cheddar instead, and you
can substitute halloumi
cheese for the talagani.

METSOVONE BITES WITH TOMATO JAM

Whisk the whole eggs and the milk together in a bowl, then add the flour and the cheeses, season with salt and pepper and mix well. Cover with plastic wrap and chill in the refrigerator for at least 5 hours until set.

Meanwhile, prepare the tomato jam. Place the tomatoes in a large heatproof bowl and pour over boiling water to cover. Leave for 1–2 minutes, then drain, cut a cross in the stem end of each tomato and peel off the skins. Chop the tomatoes.

Heat the olive oil in a small saucepan, add the onion and sweat over medium heat until soft. Add the garlic, then the chopped tomatoes, sugar, cloves, lemon juice and some salt, and stir to mix. Reduce the heat and continue cooking, stirring constantly, until the mixture has reduced to a marmalade consistency. Remove the pan from the heat and leave to cool.

Once cooled, add the basil leaves and some pepper, then transfer the mixture to a food processor or blender and blend until smooth.

Heat enough sunflower oil for deep-frying in a deep-fryer or a large, deep saucepan to 375–400°F (190–200°C). Whisk the egg whites in a bowl. Put the breadcrumbs in a separate bowl. Roll the cheese mixture into small balls, then dip them first in the egg white and then in the breadcrumbs. Deep-fry the balls in the hot oil, in batches, for about 1 minute until golden.

Drain and place on a plate lined with paper towels to soak up the excess oil. Serve hot with the tomato jam.

SAVOY CABBAGE DOLMADES WITH EGG-FREE AVGOLEMONO

This is a beloved winter dish, particularly in northern Greece where it's served on Christmas Day, as it is comforting and guaranteed to warm your heart. We have tweaked the original recipe by using Savoy cabbage leaves instead of large white cabbage leaves for stuffing with ground meat, to give the dish a splash of vivacious color. And in place of the avgolemono — egg and lemon sauce (see page 169) — that traditionally accompanies it, we have created a lemon sauce without the use of egg, which works equally well.

1 very large Savoy cabbage
    with big leaves
1 lb 2 oz (500 g) ground pork
9 oz (250 g) ground beef
5½ oz (150 g) spring onions,
    chopped
1 white onion, chopped
1 oz (30 g) short-grain or
    Arborio rice
1¾ oz (50 g) dill, chopped
4 tablespoons (60 ml) olive oil,
    plus extra for drizzling over
    the *dolmades* (or use melted
    butter)
salt and pepper
microgreens, to garnish

for the lemon sauce
3½ oz (100 g) butter
3½ oz (100 g) all-purpose flour
3⅓ cups (800 ml) vegetable
    stock
3½ oz (100 ml) freshly squeezed
    lemon juice
pinch of salt

SERVES 4

Separate the leaves of the Savoy cabbage, wash them well and then blanch them in salted boiling water until softened. Transfer them to a large bowl of ice-cold water to cool quickly, then remove, pat dry and set aside.

Put all the remaining main ingredients in a large bowl and mix thoroughly with your hands.

Use the coarsest cabbage leaves to line the base of a shallow flameproof casserole dish. Lay the remaining cabbage leaves out on a work surface with their bases nearest to you. Place about 1 tablespoon of the ground meat mixture in the center of each leaf. Fold the sides of each leaf over the filling, then tightly roll from the base of the leaf towards the top.

Place the filled and rolled cabbage leaves on top of the cabbage leaves in the casserole, sitting them next to each other in tightly packed rows. Pour in enough boiling water to cover the rolls, then drizzle with olive oil, or melted butter if you prefer. Place a large heatproof plate, upside down, on top of the rolled cabbage leaves so that they are held in place, cover with the lid and simmer for 25–30 minutes or until the cabbage leaves are soft and the ground meat is fully cooked. You may have to add a little more water if necessary.

For the lemon sauce, melt the butter in a saucepan over medium heat, add the flour and cook, whisking with a balloon whisk, until a smooth paste (roux) forms. Gradually add the stock and cook until the mixture thickens slightly, whisking constantly. Add the lemon juice and salt, then remove the pan from the heat. Pass the sauce through a fine-mesh strainer.

Pour the lemon sauce on a platter, then remove the cabbage *dolmades* from the casserole and place them on top. Garnish with microgreens and serve immediately.

SPANAKORIZOTTO

Spanakorizo — spinach risotto — is one of those dishes that is widely hated by Greek children, force fed to them by their parents because of all the health benefits it offers. Miraculously, most of us end up loving it as grown-ups.

4 tablespoons (60 ml) olive oil
1 shallot, finely chopped
11½ oz (320 g) short-grain or
   Arborio rice
1 bunch of spring onions,
   chopped
½ leek, trimmed, cleaned
   and sliced
11½ oz (320 g) spinach, washed
3–4⅓ cups (700 ml–1 liter)
   vegetable stock
1 oz (30 g) butter, diced
1½ oz (40 g) Parmesan cheese,
   grated
¾ oz (20 g) dill, chopped
½ bunch of chervil, chopped
sprinkling of chopped chives
grated zest and juice of
   1 lemon
salt and pepper
crumbled feta cheese,
   to serve

SERVES 4

Heat the olive oil in a shallow flameproof casserole dish, add the shallot and sweat over medium heat until soft but not browned. Add the rice and cook, stirring, for 1 minute. Add the spring onions, leek and spinach and cook for a further 3 minutes, stirring frequently.

Pour in 3 cups (700 ml) of the stock and cook over medium heat for 15–20 minutes, stirring occasionally, until the rice has absorbed nearly all the liquid and is al dente, adding more stock if needed.

Remove the pan from the heat and stir in the butter and Parmesan, then add all the chopped herbs. Finally, add the lemon juice and check and adjust the seasoning with salt and pepper to taste.

Divide the rice between individual bowls, crumble some feta cheese on the side and serve garnished with the grated lemon zest.

THIS IS GREAT SERVED WITH SOME FETA CHEESE OR STRAINED GREEK YOGURT.

HORTOPITA

Most people are familiar with spanakopita, the classic Greek spinach and feta pie (see page 57), but less so with hortopita, which is similar but features a combination of greens, authentically picked from the wild. This delicious superfood pie featured on our brunch menu for a while, but you can also enjoy it with your tea, for lunch or as a meze before dinner.
    If you can't find any nettles, simply make up the quantity with the other greens.

olive oil
½ leek, trimmed, cleaned
   and sliced
1 bunch of spring onions,
   chopped
1 lb 2 oz (500 g) nettles, washed
   and chopped
1 lb 2 oz (500 g) spinach,
   washed and chopped
1 lb 2 oz (500 g) cavolo nero or
   kale, washed and chopped
1 bunch of chervil, chopped
¾ oz (20 g) fennel leaves,
   chopped
1 × 8 oz (250 g) pack of filo
   pastry (12 sheets)
salt and pepper

for the cheese sauce
1¾ oz (50 g) butter
1¾ oz (50 g) all-purpose flour
18 oz (500 ml) milk
pinch of ground nutmeg
1 oz (30 g) Parmesan cheese,
   crumbled
pinch of salt
pinch of white pepper
1 egg

SERVES 6

Heat a drizzle of olive oil in a wide flameproof casserole dish, add the leek and spring onions and sauté over medium heat until softened. Add all the greens and sauté until soft, adding more olive oil as needed. Finally, stir in the chervil and fennel leaves. Remove the pan from the heat and drain the greens thoroughly in a strainer to remove as much liquid as possible. This is very important.

For the cheese sauce, melt the butter in a saucepan over medium heat, add the flour and cook, whisking with a balloon whisk, until a smooth paste (roux) forms. Gradually add the milk and cook until the mixture thickens, whisking constantly. Remove the pan from the heat and add the nutmeg, Parmesan, salt, white pepper and egg, continuing to whisk constantly.

Preheat the oven to 400°F (200°C).

Put the drained greens in a large bowl and add 9 oz (250 g) of the cheese sauce (the remainder can be frozen for use in another recipe). Mix well with your hands and check and adjust the seasoning.

Lay half the filo pastry sheets, one on top of the other, in the base of a large shallow casserole dish, about 14 x 16 inches (35 x 40 cm), brushing each with olive oil as you stack them. Add the greens mixture and spread it out into an even layer. Cover with the rest of the filo sheets, again brushing each with olive oil. Roll up the overhanging filo around the edges of the casserole dish to seal. Bake for 35–45 minutes until golden brown. Using a large sharp knife, cut the pie into equal-sized portions. Serve hot, ideally, but it's also fine warm or at room temperature.

CHICKPEA REVITHADA

This dish is our interpretation of the local speciality of the island of Sifnos in the Cyclades. It is super yummy, healthy and very easy to prepare. Try serving it with our Cured Mackerel (see page 72) on the side, and the next day you can combine any leftovers with boiled rice.

1 lb 2 oz (500 g) dried chickpeas

pinch of salt or baking soda (optional)

2 large onions, ideally grated or very finely chopped

5 oz (150 ml) extra-virgin olive oil

juice of 1 lemon, plus extra to serve

4 bay leaves

salt and pepper

SERVES 4–6

Soak the chickpeas in plenty of cold water with a pinch of salt or baking soda for at least 8 hours, preferably overnight or for 12 hours.

The next day, drain the chickpeas and rinse thoroughly. Add to a large saucepan, fill with fresh water and bring to a boil, constantly skimming off the white froth that rises to the surface. When there is no more froth, add all the remaining ingredients, seasoning with ½ teaspoon salt and a pinch of pepper. Continue boiling over medium heat for about 50 minutes until the chickpeas have softened.

Towards the end of the boiling time, preheat the oven to 400°F (200°C).

Transfer the chickpea mixture to a terracotta or ovenproof ceramic dish with a lid. Cover with the lid and bake for about 2 hours — you may need to add a little extra water once or twice. Your *revithada* is ready when the chickpeas are creamy.

Squeeze a bit of lemon juice over before serving and adjust the seasoning to your taste. A good grinding of pepper on top works well.

IN SIFNOS, REVITHADA IS A SUNDAY LUNCH TRADITION.

PERFECT FRIES

It might sound silly to some, but making perfect fries is actually not that easy. They can be too oily or too dry; overcooked or burned. But after numerous attempts, we think we have nailed the surefire recipe! They are ideal with our Filet Mignon Kontosouvli (see page 162) and Iberico Pork Chop (see page 166), but who are we kidding? On the Greek table, they go with everything!

4 large fluffy-textured
    potatoes, such as russet
sunflower oil, for deep-frying
salt

SERVES 4

Peel the potatoes and then cut them into long, thin sticks. Rinse the potato sticks in cold water until the water runs clear, then drain them thoroughly and pat them dry.

Heat enough sunflower oil for deep-frying in a deep frying pan to 375°F (190°C). Add the fries, in batches, and toss them around 2–3 times until they heat up and are well coated in oil, ensuring that they don't start to brown at this stage. Reduce the heat significantly and leave the fries to cook undisturbed for 8–12 minutes or until they become really soft.

Turn the heat up to maximum, and when the fries start turning golden, toss them around very carefully. They are ready as soon as they are golden and crisp. Turn the heat off and remove the fries with a slotted spoon.

Place them on a platter or in a bowl lined with paper towels to soak up the excess oil. Discard the paper towels, season with salt and serve immediately.

Our signature dishes are the most substantial that we serve and are mainly inspired by traditional main courses. Some of these dishes are also the most demanding in terms of the cooking techniques and effort involved, although they are still achievable for the home cook. At MAZI, as with our smaller dishes, these too are designed to be shared by the whole table, but alternatively they can be served as conventional main dishes to suit the occasion.

In this section, you will find dishes traditionally associated with celebrating Easter, such as the Slow-cooked Lamb Shank with Vegetable Briam (*see* page 179), while others like the Black Truffle Chicken Hunkar Begendi (*see* page 165) and our hearty vegetarian moussaka (*see* page 205) are perfect for any special gathering with your loved ones. The osso buco with orzo pasta (*see* page 170) makes a great Sunday lunch, while the Grilled Calamari (*see* page 187) or Braised Octopus (*see* page 198) are good choices for a summer meal.

SIGNATURE DISHES

FILET MIGNON KONTOSOUVLI WITH SMOKY TOMATOES

Kontosouvli is a spit-roasted pork dish that features on the menu of many meat eateries and grills. We have swapped the pork for filet mignon, but we serve it on metal skewers to reference the original dish.

This goes very well with a side of Perfect Fries (see page 157) and our Stir-fried Politiki Salad (see page 83).

6 large vine tomatoes
3 garlic cloves, chopped
a few oregano leaves
a few thyme leaves
a few flat-leaf parsley leaves
4 tablespoons (60 ml) olive oil,
    plus extra for drizzling over
    the steaks
4 filet mignon steaks,
    3½ oz (100 g) each
salt and pepper

to serve
Perfect Fries (see page 157)
Stir-fried Politiki Salad
    (see page 83)

SERVES 4

Preheat the oven to 400°F (200°C).

Cut the tomatoes in half and extract and discard the seeds. Place the tomatoes on a baking sheet, scatter with the garlic and herbs, drizzle with the olive oil and season with salt and pepper. Roast for 30 minutes until the tomatoes are tender yet still holding their shape.

Meanwhile, heat a griddle pan or heavy-based frying pan over a high heat until very hot. Season the fillet steaks with salt and pepper, add to the pan and drizzle with olive oil. Cook for about 5 minutes on each side for medium rare. Remove from the pan and leave to rest for 5 minutes.

Cut each steak into 3 equal-sized cubes and thread on to 4 skewers, alternating with the roasted tomatoes. Season with salt and pepper.

Serve immediately with Perfect Fries and Stir-fried Politiki Salad.

8 eggplant

olive oil

1 small onion, chopped

2 garlic cloves, finely chopped

5 boneless, skin-on chicken
   breasts

1 lb 2 oz (500 g) wild mixed
   mushrooms, cleaned and
   trimmed

drizzle of dry white wine

4 oz (120 ml) veal stock or
   demi-glace

¾ oz (20 g) butter

1 tablespoon truffle oil

1 small bunch of chives,
   chopped

salt and pepper

1 small black truffle (optional)

microgreens, to garnish

for the béchamel sauce

1 oz (25 g) butter

1 oz (25 g) all purpose flour

9 oz (250 ml) milk

pinch of ground nutmeg

pinch of salt

pinch of white pepper

SERVES 5

Another dish introduced to Greek cuisine by the Greeks of Constantinople (now Istanbul), hunkar begendi, "the sultan's delight," is usually prepared with lamb or veal. Our twist on the original, using black truffle, wild mushrooms and tender chicken breasts, has made this dish one of our biggest successes ever. The more you smoke the eggplant, the tastier the dish will be.

BLACK TRUFFLE CHICKEN HUNKAR BEGENDI

Using tongs, hold each eggplant directly over a high gas flame or electric burner on your stove, turning at intervals, for about 15 minutes until they are smoked, the skins are blackened and the flesh is soft inside. You can also chargrill them on a hot barbecue. Leave the eggplant to cool, then cut them in half lengthways and spoon out the flesh into a colander. Leave the flesh to drain for at least 2 hours.

Heat a drizzle of olive oil in a saucepan, add the onion and sweat over a gentle heat until soft but not browned. Add 1 finely chopped garlic clove and the eggplant flesh and cook, continuing to stir, until the liquid has evaporated and the mixture is a dark smoky color.

Meanwhile, for the béchamel sauce, melt the butter in a saucepan over medium heat, add the flour and cook, whisking with a balloon whisk, until a smooth paste (roux) forms. Gradually add the milk and cook until the mixture thickens, whisking constantly. Remove the pan from the heat and add the nutmeg, salt and white pepper.

Add the eggplant mixture to a food processor or blender with the béchamel sauce and blend until smooth. Preheat the oven to 400°F (200°C).

Season the chicken breasts. Heat a large, heavy-based frying pan over medium-high heat. Add a drizzle of oil and then the chicken breasts, skin side down. Cook for a few minutes until the skin has browned. Transfer to a roasting pan and cook in the oven for 20 minutes until cooked through.

While the chicken is cooking in the oven, heat a separate frying pan over high heat until smoking, add the mushrooms with a drizzle of olive oil and cook for a few minutes until the liquid they release has evaporated. Add the remaining finely chopped garlic and the white wine and stir well, then cook until the wine has evaporated. Add the veal stock or demi-glace and cook until reduced and the mixture becomes thick and sticky. Finally, stir in the butter, truffle oil and chopped chives.

Place the chicken breasts on top of the eggplant purée and arrange the mushrooms and their cooking juices alongside. Grate over the truffle, if using, and garnish with microgreens.

CARAMELIZED IBERICO PORK CHOP

We choose this world-renowned Spanish speciality pork for its superb taste and tenderness, but then we cook it the Greek way with oregano, olive oil and lemon. We recommend that you don't trim the chops, as the fat infuses the meat to give it an incomparable flavor. If you are unable to source Iberico pork chops, buy the best-quality free-range bone-in pork chops you can find. Serve with some Perfect Fries (see page 157).

4 Iberico pork chops
olive oil, for brushing
3½ oz (100 ml) extra-virgin olive oil
juice of 1 lemon
pinch of dried oregano
salt and pepper
Perfect Fries (see page 157), to serve

for the brine
6⅓ cups (1.5 liters) water
4¼ oz (120 g) sea salt flakes
1¾ oz (50 g) superfine sugar
1 bay leaf
5 black peppercorns
4 sprigs of thyme
1 small carrot, peeled and diced
1 celery stick, sliced
1 small onion, sliced
3 garlic cloves, crushed

SERVES 4

First prepare the brine. Pour the measured water into a deep pan that is large enough to accommodate the chops but small enough to fit in the refrigerator. Add the salt and sugar and heat over medium heat, stirring, until they have dissolved. Remove from the heat, add all the remaining brine ingredients and leave to cool completely.

Add the pork chops to the brine and leave to soak in the refrigerator for 2 hours. Remove from the brine and wash them thoroughly with cold water, then pat dry with paper towels.

Heat an indoor grill if you have one until hot, or use an outdoor barbecue. Brush the pork chops on both sides with the olive oil, add to the hot barbecue or grill and cook for 8–10 minutes on each side until cooked through. If you don't have a grill or barbecue, preheat the oven to 400°F (200°C). Heat a griddle pan or large, heavy-based frying pan over medium-high heat, add the oiled chops and cook for 4–5 minutes on each side. Transfer to a baking sheet and finish cooking in the oven for 18–20 minutes until cooked through.

While the chops are cooking, mix the extra-virgin olive oil with the lemon juice, oregano and a pinch of salt in a bowl.

To serve, season the chops with salt and pepper, thinly slice and then pour the lemon oil over the top. Serve with Perfect Fries.

THIS IS ALSO GREAT SERVED WITH OUR STIR-FRIED POLITIKI SALAD (SEE PAGE 83).

LAMB FRICASSÉE

The term "fricassée" is usually used to refer to the classic French method of cooking meat "halfway between a sauté and a stew," as described by Julia Child. However, in Greek cuisine it is applied to this very traditional dish of tender braised lamb, lettuce, dill and spring onions in an avgolemono sauce.

4 heads of romaine lettuce,
    each cut into 3
1 oz (25 g) butter
4 lb 8 oz (2 kg) boneless lamb
    shoulder, cut into chunks
6 bunches of spring onions,
    chopped
2 bunches of dill, finely
    chopped
1 bunch of flat-leaf parsley,
    finely chopped
salt and pepper

for the avgolemono sauce
2 eggs
juice of 2 lemons

SERVES 6

Wash the lettuce thoroughly, then blanch in boiling water for 3 minutes. Drain and set aside.

Melt the butter in a large flameproof casserole dish, add the lamb and sauté over medium heat until browned. Add the spring onions, dill, parsley and lettuce, season with salt and pepper and very briefly sauté. Add enough water to cover the meat, cover with the lid and cook over low heat for 1½ hours until cooked through and falling apart.

For the *avgolemono* sauce, beat the eggs and lemon juice together in a bowl with a little of the liquid from the casserole, then pour the egg mixture into the casserole and stir slowly so that it is evenly distributed. Serve immediately.

GIOUVETSI WITH BRAISED OSSO BUCO

Giouvetsi is an oven-baked dish of orzo, a pasta that resembles rice, usually combined with chicken or lamb, tomato sauce and lots of spices. We use pieces of veal shank (shin), commonly known as osso buco, instead, for their tenderness, and rather than simply combining all the elements and baking together in the oven, we cook the orzo like a risotto. This way all the delicious juices are retained, without the risk of the dish drying up.

Myzithra or mizythra is an unpasteurized cheese that has been made from the whey of sheep, goat or cow milk in Greece for thousands of years. There are two forms of myzithra: fresh, which is unsalted and consumed within a few days, and dry, where the cheese is aged to a rock-hard texture and usually used for grating over pasta. If you can't get it, use Parmesan.

SERVES 6

4 pieces of veal shank, about
    7 oz (200 g) each
all-purpose flour, for sprinkling
olive oil
2 carrots, peeled and diced
2 shallots, sliced
1 celery stick, sliced
1 small leek, trimmed, cleaned
    and sliced
4 garlic cloves, halved
5 sprigs of thyme
2 tablespoons tomato purée
14 oz (400 ml) red wine
14 oz (400 ml) dry white wine
pinch of sweet paprika
3 cloves
pinch of ground cinnamon
salt and pepper

Preheat the oven to 400°F (200°C).

Season the veal pieces with salt and pepper, then sprinkle them with flour, shaking off any excess.

Heat a drizzle of olive oil in a large saucepan over medium-high heat and sear the veal pieces for 3–5 minutes on each side until browned. Remove and reserve in a roasting pan.

Replace the oil in the veal pan with a fresh drizzle. Add the carrots, shallots, celery, leek, garlic and thyme and sauté over medium heat for 8–10 minutes until the vegetables have softened. Add the tomato purée and both wines, then stir in the spices and bring to a boil. Once starting to boil, transfer the contents of the pan to the roasting pan. Pour in enough water to fill the pan by about three-quarters or to just cover the veal pieces, then cover the pan with foil and cook in the oven for 1–1½ hours until cooked through.

Remove from the oven (but keep it on at the same temperature for roasting the tomatoes), lift the veal pieces out of the pan and cut each into 4 strips. Pass the sauce through a strainer into a saucepan and cook over high heat until reduced by half. Set aside.

RECIPE CONTINUES...

for the tomato sauce

20 cherry tomatoes, halved
pinch of sugar
2 garlic cloves, halved
4 sprigs of thyme
olive oil, for drizzling

for the orzo pasta

drizzle of olive oil
½ shallot, chopped
½ carrot, peeled and finely
    diced
¼ celery root, finely diced
1 garlic clove, finely chopped
1 lb 12 oz (800 g) dried orzo
    pasta
drizzle of dry white wine
6⅓ cups (1.5 liters) chicken
    stock (you might not need
    all of it)
1 oz (25 g) butter
½ bunch of chives, finely
    chopped
1¾ oz (50 g) dry myzithra
    cheese, grated, to serve

Meanwhile, for the tomato sauce, spread the tomato halves out on a baking sheet. Sprinkle over the sugar, some salt, the garlic and thyme sprigs and drizzle with olive oil. Roast for 15–20 minutes. Remove from the oven, then tip the roasted tomatoes and garlic into a food processor or blender, discarding the thyme sprigs, and blend until puréed.

For the orzo pasta, heat the olive oil in a saucepan and sweat the shallot, carrot and celeriac over medium heat for 6 minutes until soft. Add the garlic, orzo and white wine and simmer until the wine has evaporated. Cover the orzo with half the stock and half the reduced sauce from the osso buco, then simmer for 15–20 minutes until the pasta is al dente and the sauce is thick. You may need to add a little more of the stock and osso buco sauce. Stir in 2–3 tablespoons of the roasted tomato sauce, the butter and chives, then check and adjust the seasoning if necessary.

To serve, divide the orzo pasta between serving bowls, sprinkle with the grated myzithra cheese and place the osso bucos on top.

ONE OF OUR MOST POPULAR DISHES, THIS HAS INSPIRED MANY OTHER GREEK RESTAURANTS.

3 lb 5 oz (1.5 kg) pork cheeks
olive oil
1 onion, sliced
2 garlic cloves, crushed
1 carrot, peeled and sliced
1 celery stick, sliced
1 tablespoon tomato purée
14 oz (400 ml) red wine
6⅓ cups (1.5 liters) water
5 sprigs of thyme

for the brine

8½ cups (2 liters) water
3¾ oz (110 g) rock salt
2¼ oz (65 g) superfine sugar
1 carrot, peeled and sliced
1 celery, sliced
handful of black peppercorns
3 garlic cloves, crushed
3 bay leaves
4 sprigs of thyme

for the artichoke lemon
cream

1 tablespoon olive oil, plus
    extra for sweating the
    vegetables
1 small white onion, sliced
1 leek, white part only,
    trimmed, cleaned and sliced
1 lb (450g) fresh artichoke
    hearts (see page 132), or
    frozen artichoke hearts,
    defrosted, quartered
½ medium potato, cooked in
    boiling water until soft, then
    drained and halved again
20 oz (600 ml) vegetable stock
½ oz (15 g) unsalted butter
juice of ½ lemon
salt and pepper

BRAISED PORK CHEEKS WITH GLOBE AND JERUSALEM ARTICHOKES

First prepare the brine. Pour the measured water into a deep pan that is large enough to accommodate the pork cheeks but small enough to fit in the refrigerator. Add the rock salt and sugar and heat over medium heat, stirring, until they have dissolved. Remove from the heat, add all the remaining brine ingredients and leave to cool completely.

Add the pork cheeks to the brine and leave to soak in the refrigerator for 2 hours. Remove from the brine and wash them thoroughly with cold water, then pat dry with paper towels.

Preheat the oven to 375°F (190°C).

Heat a large, heavy based frying pan over medium-high heat, add a drizzle of oil and the pork cheeks and brown on each side. Transfer them to a roasting pan. Replace the oil in the pan with a fresh drizzle, add the onion and garlic and sauté over medium heat until softened but not browned. Add the carrot and celery and sauté until softened. Add the tomato purée, red wine, measured water and thyme sprigs and simmer for another 10 minutes. Transfer to the roasting pan with the pork cheeks, cover with foil and bake for 1½ hours until cooked through.

Meanwhile, prepare the artichoke lemon cream. Heat a drizzle of olive oil in a saucepan, add the onion and leek and sweat over medium heat until soft. Add the artichoke hearts and cooked potato, cover with the vegetable stock and simmer until the artichokes are soft and the potato has completely disintegrated. Remove from the heat, strain the vegetables from the stock and add them to a food processor or blender with the butter, 1 tablespoon olive oil and lemon juice. Blend until smooth, then check and season to taste.

RECIPE CONTINUES...

for the Jerusalem artichokes in milk

7 Jerusalem artichokes, peeled and quartered
18 oz (500 ml) milk
2 sprigs of thyme
1 bay leaf
a little butter, for glazing
a pinch of salt
a few black peppercorns

for the Jerusalem artichoke chips

3 Jerusalem artichokes
rapeseed oil, for frying

For the Jerusalem artichokes in milk, put the Jerusalem artichokes in a saucepan with the milk, thyme sprigs and bay leaf and season with a pinch each of salt and pepper. Bring to a boil and cook until soft. Remove from the milk and set aside.

For the Jerusalem artichoke chips, heat enough rapeseed oil for deep-frying in a deep-fryer or a large, deep saucepan to 375°F (190°C). Wash the unpeeled artichokes and pat dry, then finely slice — use a mandolin if you have one. Deep-fry in the hot oil for about 1 minute until golden. Drain and place on a plate lined with paper towels to soak up the excess oil. Sprinkle with salt.

When the pork cheeks are ready, remove them from the roasting pan and set aside. Pass the sauce through a strainer into a saucepan. Simmer briskly to reduce the sauce until it is thick, then add the pork cheeks and turn in the sauce to glaze them.

To finish the artichokes in milk, add them to a saucepan over medium heat and gently turn in a little butter, just enough to glaze them, seasoning with the salt and peppercorns.

To serve, add some of the artichoke cream to the plate and place the glazed pork cheeks on top. Arrange the artichokes in milk on the plate and finally add the artichoke chips.

Pork cheek is a cut of meat that is often misunderstood or overlooked, but it's worth going out of your way to source it, as it has a superbly silky texture, so smooth and sublime that it melts in your mouth. Paired with both artichoke hearts and Jerusalem artichokes, they make an exquisite dish.

SLOW-COOKED LAMB SHANK WITH VEGETABLE BRIAM

This first appeared on the MAZI menu as our Easter special but remained there until September due to popular demand. We guarantee that this dish will bring spring to your dining table too.

Briam is a Greek vegetable dish similar to ratatouille but baked in the oven and is usually made during the summer to take advantage of the abundance of ripe vegetables, served with some feta on the side. Greek basil has a bushy growing habit with small, highly aromatic leaves, spicy and clove-like in flavor. A common sight throughout the Cyclades Islands, terracotta pots of Greek basil are placed on tables as a sign of welcome and to fill the air with an inviting fragrance.

SERVES 6

6 lamb shanks
olive oil
1 large carrot, peeled and
    roughly sliced
1 white onion, roughly sliced
2 celery sticks, roughly sliced
4 garlic cloves, halved
5 sprigs of thyme
2 bay leaves
2 tablespoons tomato purée
2 ripe tomatoes, grated
18 oz (500 ml) port
18 oz (500 ml) red wine
pinch of sweet paprika
4 cloves
2 pinches of ground cinnamon
salt and pepper

Preheat the oven to 400°F (200°C).

Season the lamb shanks with salt and pepper. Heat a drizzle of olive oil in a large saucepan over medium-high heat and sear the lamb shanks for 3–5 minutes on each side until browned. Transfer them to a roasting pan.

Replace the oil in the lamb pan with a fresh drizzle. Add the carrot, onion, celery, garlic, thyme sprigs and bay leaves and sauté over medium heat for 8–10 minutes until the vegetables have softened.

Add the tomato purée, tomatoes, port and red wine, then stir in the spices and bring to a boil. Once starting to boil, transfer the contents of the saucepan to the roasting pan. Pour in enough water to fill the tray by about three-quarters or to just cover the lamb shanks, then cover the tray with foil and cook in the oven for 2 hours.

RECIPE CONTINUES...

for the vegetable briam

extra-virgin olive oil
1 white onion, sliced
1 leek, white part only, trimmed,
    cleaned and sliced
1 eggplant, diced
2 zucchini, deseeded
    and diced
1 large red pepper, cored,
    deseeded and diced
1 large green pepper, cored,
    deseeded and diced
2 garlic cloves, finely chopped
5 sprigs of thyme
10½ oz (300 g) good-quality
    canned chopped tomatoes
½ bunch of Greek basil,
    chopped
½ bunch of flat-leaf parsley,
    chopped

Meanwhile, for the vegetable *briam*, heat a drizzle of extra-virgin olive oil in a large saucepan, add the onion and cook over medium heat until soft and caramelized. Add the leek and very briefly sauté, stirring. Then add the eggplant with a little more olive oil, followed by the zucchini, peppers and garlic and again briefly sauté. Season with salt and add the thyme sprigs.

Pour in the chopped tomatoes with a little water and cook over medium heat for 15–20 minutes until the vegetables are cooked and the sauce has thickened, adding extra water if needed. Stir in the chopped Greek basil and parsley, and check and adjust the seasoning.

Remove the roasting pan from the oven, then lift out the lamb shanks and set aside. Pass the sauce through a strainer into a saucepan and cook over high heat until you have a thick sauce. Return the lamb shanks to the sauce, mix well and warm through.

Serve the lamb shanks and sauce hot with the vegetable *briam* on the side.

ROOSTER PASTITSADA WITH TRUFFLE OIL AND GRAVIERA CREAM

The inspiration for this dish came from Corfu's local speciality pastitsada, which often consists of beef or cockerel (rooster), a secret mix of spices (spetsieriko), thick long pasta and shaved kefalotyri (or kefalotiri), a hard, salty white cheese made from sheep or goat milk in Greece and Cyprus. We opted for the rooster and added a truffle and a graviera cheese cream. Needless to say, it became our new hit dish straight away.

If you can't find graviera cheese (see page 29), use Gruyère instead.

SERVES 6

microgreens, to garnish

for the pasta
9 oz (250 g) 00 flour,
    plus extra for dusting
4½ oz (125 g) egg yolks
1 oz (25 g) egg whites
olive oil, for drizzling

for the rooster
2 lb 4 oz (1 kg) whole oven-
    ready cockerel
1 large carrot, peeled and
    roughly chopped
2 celery sticks, roughly
    chopped
1 white onion, roughly chopped
2 bay leaves
handful of black peppercorns
1 bunch of chives, chopped
1 bunch of flat-leaf parsley,
    chopped
drizzle of truffle oil, plus extra
    to serve
1¾ oz (50 g) Parmesan cheese,
    grated
salt

For the pasta, put all the ingredients except the olive oil in the bowl of a stand mixer fitted with the dough hook and mix on low speed until the mixture forms a dough. Alternatively, knead the ingredients together in a bowl with your hands until a dough is formed. Cover the dough with plastic wrap and leave to rest for 2–3 hours in the refrigerator.

For the rooster, fill a large saucepan with water and add some salt. Add the cockerel, all the vegetables, the bay leaves and peppercorns and bring to a boil, then reduce the heat to low and gently simmer for 2 hours until cooked through. Lift the cockerel from the water and leave until cool enough to handle, then remove all the meat from the bones, discarding the skin. Strain the stock, discarding the solids, into a saucepan, add the meat and simmer for 1 hour until all the liquid has evaporated but the meat is still juicy.

Meanwhile, for the tomato sauce, heat the oil in a separate saucepan, add the onion and garlic and sauté over medium heat until softened but not browned. Grate the tomatoes and add these to the pan with the sugar. Season with the salt, pepper and spices and simmer until the mixture has thickened to a sauce consistency.

Roll the pasta dough out on a floured work surface until very thin. If you have a pasta machine, roll the dough out until about ¼ inch (5 mm) thick, then fold in half and pass through the machine on its widest setting. Repeat the folding and rolling process several times until the dough is shiny. Then pass the sheet of dough through the machine, working down through the settings, from the widest setting to the second thinnest. Use a 4½-inch (12 cm) round cutter to cut the dough into rounds.

RECIPE CONTINUES...

for the tomato sauce

drizzle of olive oil
½ onion, chopped
1 garlic clove, chopped
2 lb 4 oz (1 kg) ripe tomatoes,
    halved, seeds discarded
2 pinches of sugar
pinch of salt
pinch of pepper
pinch of sweet paprika
pinch of ground cumin
pinch of ground cinnamon

for the graviera cream

3½ oz (100 g) graviera cheese,
    grated
3½ oz (100 g) Parmesan cheese,
    grated
20 oz (600 ml) heavy cream
¾ oz (20 g) cornstarch
salt and pepper

For the graviera cream, put the cheeses in a saucepan with the cream and bring to a simmer, stirring constantly, until they have melted. Season with salt and pepper. Mix the cornstarch with a little cold water to make a smooth paste, then stir into the cream mixture and cook gently, stirring, until thickened. Pass through a strainer and add to a cream whipping siphon, if you have one, charging the canister with a nitrous oxide (N_2O) cartridge according to the manufacturer's instructions. Shake well and set aside somewhere warm.

Add the cockerel to a bowl with 10½ oz (300 g) of the tomato sauce and mix together well. Add the chopped chives and parsley, then drizzle with the truffle oil and sprinkle with the grated Parmesan.

Cook the rounds of pasta in a large saucepan of boiling water for 1 minute, then drain and drizzle with some olive oil so that they don't stick together.

Layer the rounds of pasta with the cockerel mixture in serving bowls, then dispense or spoon over the graviera cream and drizzle with some more truffle oil. Garnish with microgreens and serve immediately.

REPLACE
THE COCKEREL
WITH CHICKEN
IF YOU PREFER.

1 lb 2 oz (500 g) Brussels
    sprouts
6 skinless halibut fillets,
    3½ oz (100 g) each
2 pinches of salt
extra-virgin olive oil
1 teaspoon peeled and finely
    chopped fresh root ginger
grated zest of 1 lemon
pepper
sprinkling of microgreens,
    to garnish

for the avgolemono *sauce*
18 oz (500 ml) vegetable stock
6 eggs
7 oz (200 ml) heavy cream
7 oz (200 g) unsalted butter,
    diced
juice of 6 lemons
pinch of salt
pinch of pepper

SERVES 6

Avgolemono is a
traditional Greek sauce
made with eggs and
lemon, which usually
accompanies winter meat
dishes and soups. We have
instead paired it with fish
and Brussels sprouts for
an unusual take on the
original that works really
well. This is a quick and
easy dish to prepare but
one that is big on flavor
and health benefits.

HALIBUT WITH BRUSSELS SPROUTS AND AVGOLEMONO SAUCE

Separate each Brussels sprout into leaves, peeling them off one by one.
Set aside.

For the *avgolemono* sauce, heat the vegetable stock in a saucepan, add the
eggs and cream to the hot stock and blend with an immersion blender. Bring
to a boil over medium heat and cook, whisking constantly, until the mixture
thickens. Add the butter, lemon juice and the salt and pepper and continue
cooking, whisking constantly, until it thickens again. Remove the pan from
the heat and pass the mixture through a fine-mesh strainer into a bowl.

Heat a heavy-based frying pan over high heat. Season the halibut fillets with
the salt and some pepper. Drizzle 1 tablespoon of olive oil into the hot pan,
then add the halibut fillets and sear for 2 minutes on each side, until both
sides are golden brown.

Meanwhile, in a separate frying pan, heat a drizzle of olive oil over medium
heat, add the Brussels sprout leaves and sauté for 30 seconds.
Add the ginger and lemon zest and sauté for a further 30 seconds.

Divide the Brussels sprout leaves between 6 dishes and top with the
halibut fillets. Pour the warm *avgolemono* sauce around and sprinkle
with the microgreens.

1 quantity of Black-eyed
    Bean Salad (*see* page 82)
6 medium-sized baby squid
    (calamari), cleaned and
    heads/tentacles and
    bodies separated
olive oil, or sunflower oil
    if deep-frying
juice of 1 lemon
salt

for the spinach purée
4 teaspoons olive oil
2 teaspoons butter
1 bunch of spring onions,
    chopped
1 garlic clove, chopped
8½ oz (240 g) baby spinach
    leaves, washed
½ bunch of dill, chopped
3½ oz (100 ml) water
salt and pepper

for the chive oil
3½ oz (100 ml) extra-virgin
    olive oil
1 garlic clove, crushed
grated zest of 1 lemon
grated zest of 1 lime
1 small red chili, finely chopped
½ bunch of chives, finely
    chopped

SERVES 6

This is one of those
dishes that instantly
brings Greece to the mind.
It's vital for this recipe to
source fresh rather than
frozen squid, and the best
quality you can find.

GRILLED CALAMARI WITH BLACK-EYED BEANS AND SPINACH PURÉE

First of all, follow the instructions on page 82 to prepare the black-eyed bean salad.

For the spinach purée, heat the olive oil and 1 teaspoon of the butter in a saucepan, add the spring onions and garlic and sweat over medium heat until soft but not browned. Add the spinach and dill, season with salt and pepper and cook until the spinach has wilted.

Transfer the spinach mixture to a food processor or blender, add the measured water and remaining teaspoon of butter and blend until puréed. Pour the purée into a bowl and place the bowl on top of another bowl filled with ice-cold water in order to keep the purée a nice bright green color.

Mix all the ingredients for the chive oil together in a bowl and set aside.

Heat a griddle pan or heavy-based frying pan over high heat — you can use a barbecue in the summer months or an indoor grill if you have one. Cut the squid bodies into pieces and season with salt. Add the squid to the hot pan with a drizzle of olive oil and cook for 1 minute on each side until the squid firm up, turn from opaque to white inside and are nicely charred. Repeat with the squid heads/tentacles. Alternatively, deep-fry the squid heads/tentacles in a large, deep saucepan or a deep-fryer in sunflower oil heated to 375–400°F (190–200°C) for 1 minute, then drain and place on a plate lined with paper towels to soak up the excess oil. Squeeze the lemon juice over the calamari.

To serve, spread the spinach purée on a plate and pile the black-eyed bean salad on top. Add the calamari bodies and drizzle them with the chive oil, then place the calamari heads/tentacles on top.

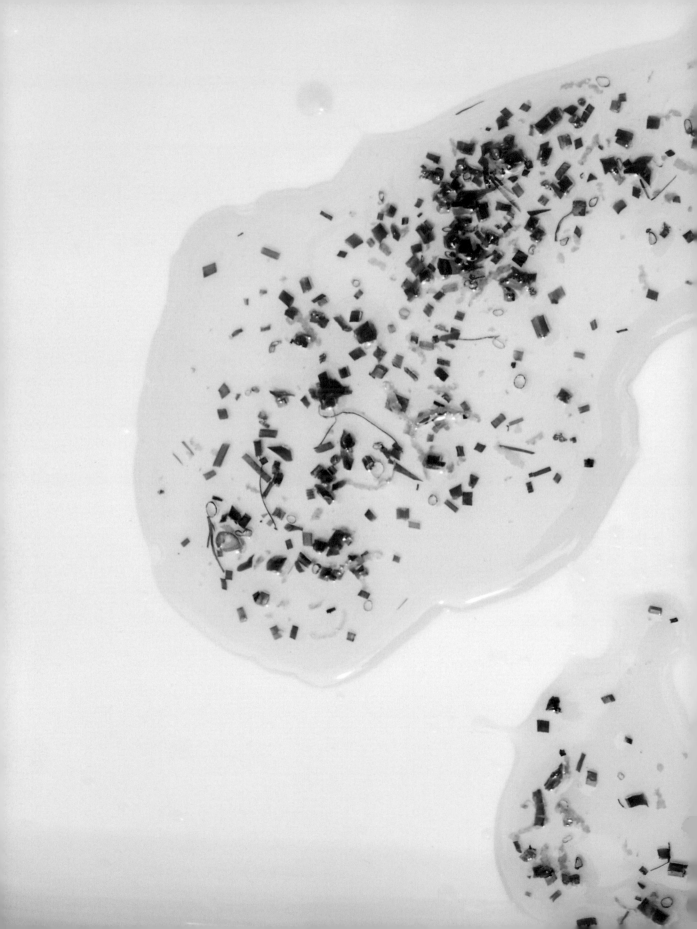

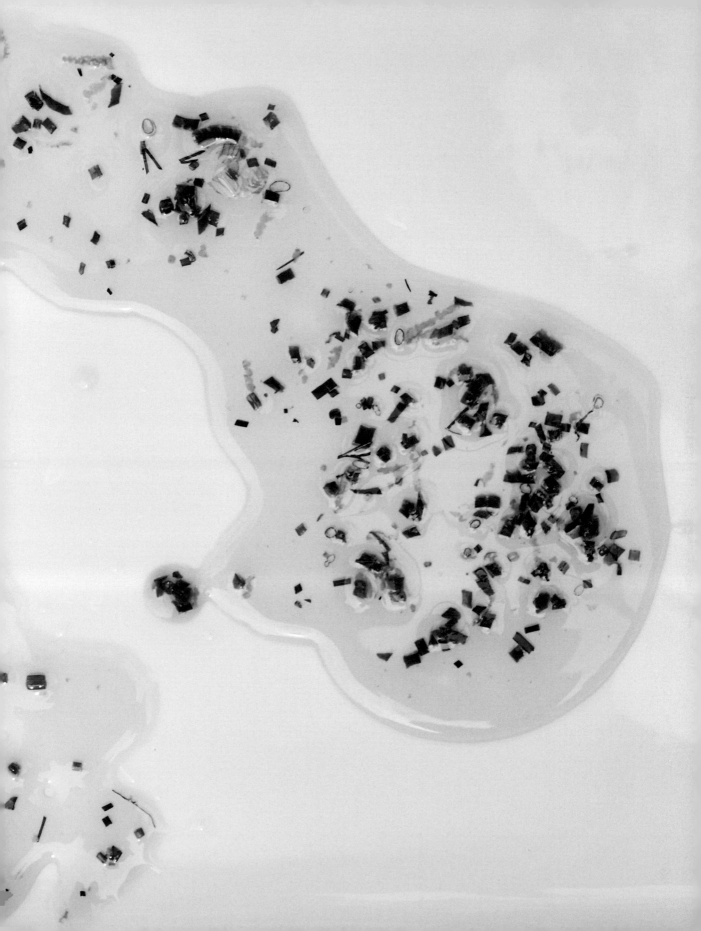

WILD COD WITH BLACK GARLIC SKORDALIA AND POTATO RÖSTI

Greeks mark their major national holiday, March 25, in food terms by eating salt-battered cod with skordalia, fries and beet salad. We took inspiration from that tradition and created this contemporary dish — a perfect example of what MAZI is all about.

3 large raw beets
extra-virgin olive oil
4 teaspoons red wine vinegar
4 skinless wild cod fillets,
    4½ oz (125 g) each
½ quantity of Skordalia with
    Black Garlic (*see* page 47)
salt
basil leaves, to garnish

for the potato rösti
2 large russet potatoes
1½ oz (40 g) unsalted butter
drizzle of sunflower oil

SERVES 4

Put the beets in a large saucepan and cover with cold water, then add a drizzle of olive oil and the vinegar. Bring to a boil and cook over medium heat for about 20 minutes, depending on their size, or until they are cooked through and soft. Drain them and leave to cool. Peel off the skins, then cut into dice. Season with salt.

Preheat the oven to 400°F (200°C).

For the potato rösti, peel the potatoes, then coarsely grate on to a clean kitchen towel, gather the kitchen towel around the potato to form a bag and squeeze to remove as much moisture as possible.

Line a baking sheet with parchment paper. Heat a heavy-based frying pan over medium-high heat. Season the cod fillets with salt, add to the hot pan with a drizzle of olive oil and fry for 2 minutes on each side. Transfer to the lined baking sheet and cook in the oven for a further 5–6 minutes until firm and opaque.

While the cod is cooking, heat the butter and sunflower oil for the rösti in a large frying pan over medium heat and place a 3½-inch (9 cm) stainless steel cooking ring in the pan. Fill with a quarter of the grated potato (but not too deeply), then remove the ring. Repeat with the rest of the grated potato. Fry the rösti for 3–4 minutes on each side, adding more oil if needed, until golden brown all over and cooked through. Drain and place on a plate lined with paper towels, then season with salt.

To serve, spread the black garlic *skordalia* on each plate and place a potato rosti on top. Add some diced beets alongside each rosti, then top with a cod fillet. Garnish with basil leaves and serve immediately.

FRESH CALAMARI RICELESS RISOTTO WITH ARUGULA PESTO

This dish has left many of our guests confounded as to how a risotto can be riceless. The trick is that we dice the calamari really finely to make it look like risotto, so there truly is no rice involved at all. This recipe will make more pesto than you will need. You can store the remainder in a clean, airtight jar or container in the refrigerator for up to 3 days.

2 lb 4 oz (1 kg) medium-sized
    baby squid (calamari),
    cleaned and heads/tentacles
    and bodies separated
sunflower oil, for deep-frying
juice of 1 lemon
drizzle of olive oil
salt and pepper

for the arugula pesto
10 oz (280 g) arugula
6¼ oz (180 g) pine nuts
3 garlic cloves, peeled
5½ oz (150 g) Parmesan cheese,
    grated
7 oz (200 ml) extra-virgin olive
    oil
2 ice cubes
pinch of salt
pinch of pepper

for the tempura batter
7 oz (200 g) store-bought
    tempura batter mix
10 oz (300 ml) cold water

SERVES 8

First make the arugula pesto. Put all the ingredients in a food processor or blender and blend until very smooth. Transfer to a bowl, cover and chill in the refrigerator for an hour.

Whisk the tempura batter mix with the measured water in a separate bowl, then cover and leave to rest in the refrigerator for at least 10 minutes.

Meanwhile, very finely dice the squid bodies.

Heat enough sunflower oil for deep-frying in a deep-fryer or a large, deep saucepan to 375°F (190°C). Dip the calamari heads/tentacles into the tempura batter and deep-fry in the hot oil for 1–2 minutes until golden and crisp. Drain and place on a plate lined with paper towels to soak up the excess oil. Squeeze over the lemon juice.

Heat a large, heavy-based frying pan over high heat until smoking. Add the olive oil and then the diced squid and fry, stirring, for about 1 minute. Add 6 tablespoons of the arugula pesto and cook, continuing to stir, for another minute until the mixture is well blended and smooth. Season with salt and pepper if needed.

Serve the calamari immediately, topped with the deep-fried calamari heads/tentacles.

LOBSTER PASTA WITH METAXA AND BASIL

Lobster pasta was invented on the small north Aegean island of Skyros, often dubbed "lobster island." In the old days, the island fishermen would take home the lobsters that were beaten up through fighting with each other and therefore couldn't be sold to feed their families. But how could a couple of lobsters satisfy the hunger of a six-member family? That's when they came up with the idea of mixing the lobster meat with pasta to make a substantial meal out of it, and thus a wonderful dish was born!

You need to use freshly killed uncooked lobsters for this dish rather than cooked, which are available in the fresh fish department at most supermarkets.

5½ tablespoons (80 ml) extra-virgin olive oil, plus extra to finish the sauce (or use 2–3 tablespoons of butter)
2 garlic cloves, chopped
¼ oz (10 g) sprigs of thyme
2 medium uncooked lobsters, 1 lb 2 oz–1 lb 12 oz (500–800 g) each, cut in half lengthways and cleaned
4 teaspoons Metaxa 5 star brandy (or other brandy)
1 lb 2 oz (500 g) dried capellini or linguine pasta
¼ oz (10 g) Greek basil, chopped
¼ oz (10 g) flat-leaf parsley, chopped
salt and pepper

for the lobster stock
14 oz (400 g) lobster shells
1 onion, chopped
1 celery stick, sliced
1 carrot, peeled and sliced
2 tablespoons Metaxa 5 star brandy (or other brandy)
4 oz (125 ml) dry white wine
1 tablespoon tomato purée

SERVES 4

First make the lobster stock. Preheat the oven to 425°F (220°C). Place the lobster shells, onion, celery and carrot in a roasting pan and roast for 10–15 minutes.

Meanwhile, add the brandy to a large saucepan and simmer briskly until almost all has evaporated, then add the white wine and again reduce almost to nothing. Stir in the tomato purée and add the roasted lobster shells and vegetables, cover with water and simmer for 1½ hours, skimming off any white foam that rises to the surface. Pass the stock through a fine-mesh strainer and set aside.

Heat the olive oil in a large saucepan over medium heat, add the garlic and thyme and briefly sauté without browning the garlic. Add the lobsters and pour in the brandy. Add a good ladle of the lobster stock, cover with a lid, bring to a boil, and then reduce the heat and simmer for 5–8 minutes.

Meanwhile, cook the pasta in a large saucepan of salted boiling water according to the packet instructions until al dente. Just before the pasta is ready, remove the lobsters from their sauce and break them into pieces, using kitchen scissors if you need to.

Strain the pasta and add to the sauce along with a splash of the pasta cooking water. Finish the sauce with a drizzle of olive oil or 2–3 tablespoons of butter, the chopped basil and parsley and a good grinding of pepper.

Serve the pasta immediately, topped with the lobster pieces.

BRAISED OCTOPUS WITH GARDEN HERB POTATO SALAD AND YUZU LADOLEMONO

This recipe is all about successfully rendering the octopus beautifully tender. The usual trick to achieving that in Greece is to smash the freshly landed octopus repeatedly against a rock or wall. But have no fear, we suggest an easier method!

Ladolemono is the classic Greek dressing of lemon and olive oil used for fish, seafood and salads, but here we have replaced the lemon with yuzu, a Japanese citrus fruit, for an interesting Asian twist.

SERVES 8

1 large octopus, cleaned

3½ oz (100 ml) olive oil, plus an extra drizzle for frying the octopus

2 oz (50 ml) red wine vinegar

2 oz (50 ml) white balsamic vinegar

3 garlic cloves, halved

grated zest and juice of 2 lemons, plus extra juice for drizzling over the fried octopus

grated zest of 2 limes

10 black peppercorns

½ bunch of thyme

pinch of dried oregano, plus extra for sprinkling over the fried octopus

4 bay leaves

steamed samphire, to serve

Preheat the oven to 425°F (220°C).

Cut the tentacles from the head of the octopus and put them straight into a large, dry saucepan over high heat. Cook for a couple of minutes until the octopus has released some of its liquid, then drain off the liquid. Repeat this process 2–3 times.

Transfer the octopus tentacles to a roasting pan and add all the remaining ingredients for the octopus. Mix together well, then cover with foil. Braise in the oven for 30–45 minutes. Remove from the oven, strain the tentacles, discarding the braising liquid, and set aside.

RECIPE CONTINUES...

for the potato salad

5 lb 8 oz (2.5 kg) fluffy-textured
    potatoes, such as russet
1 roasted red pepper from a jar,
    drained, diced
7 oz (200 g) pitted Kalamata
    olives, chopped
1 small red onion, chopped
½ bunch of spring onions,
    chopped
1 small bunch of chives,
    chopped
1 small bunch of flat-leaf
    parsley, chopped
1 tablespoon Dijon mustard
juice of 1 lime
salt and pepper

for the yuzu ladolemono

3½ oz (100 ml) yuzu juice
1 tablespoon Dijon mustard
10 oz (300 ml) extra-virgin olive
    oil
salt and pepper

Meanwhile, for the potato salad, cook the potatoes in a large saucepan of boiling water until soft when you pierce them — how long this takes will very much depend on the size of the potatoes. Drain and leave to cool, then peel off the skins. Finely chop the potatoes and then mix with all the remaining potato salad ingredients in a large bowl.

Put all the ingredients for the yuzu *ladolemono* in a bowl and blend with an immersion blender if you want a thick dressing, or lightly beat together with a fork.

Cut each octopus tentacle into 4 pieces. Heat a large, heavy-based frying pan over medium-high heat, add a drizzle of olive oil and fry the octopus pieces for a couple of minutes until crispy. Remove from the pan and drizzle with a little lemon juice and sprinkle with dried oregano.

Press the potato salad into a pastry ring on a plate to create a perfect circle. Remove the ring, then arrange the fried octopus pieces on top. Smear the yuzu *ladolemono* on the edge of the plate and serve accompanied by steamed samphire.

SHIITAKE MUSHROOM AND POTATO DAUPHINOISE MOUSSAKA

Moussaka is one Greek dish that doesn't need much introduction. But we have given the traditional recipe a fresh treatment by substituting shiitake mushrooms for the ground beef, turning it into a great vegetarian dish. These mushrooms have such a "meaty" texture that people often can't quite believe that the dish is indeed meat free.

SERVES 6

2 large eggplant, peeled
sunflower oil, for deep-frying
drizzle of olive oil
1 shallot, chopped
1 garlic clove, chopped
10½ oz (300 g) shiitake
   mushrooms, sliced
3 sprigs of thyme
2 oz (50 ml) dry white wine
1 tablespoon tomato purée
9 oz (250 g) good-quality
   canned chopped tomatoes
pinch of sugar
pinch of ground cloves
pinch of sweet paprika
pinch of ground cinnamon
1¾ oz (50 g) Parmesan cheese,
   grated
salt and pepper

for the dauphinoise
4 baking potatoes
2 oz (50 ml) milk
3½ oz (100 g) Parmesan cheese,
   grated
3½ oz (100 ml) heavy cream

Cut the eggplant into thick slices. Put them in a colander, sprinkle with a generous pinch of salt and leave them to drain for 30 minutes.

Heat enough sunflower oil for deep-frying in a deep-fryer or a large, deep saucepan to 375°F (190°C). Pat the eggplant slices dry with paper towels and deep-fry, in batches, for 1 minute until soft. Drain and place on a plate lined with paper towels to soak up the excess oil.

For the dauphinoise, preheat the oven to 400°F (200°C).

Peel the potatoes and then thinly slice them — use a mandolin if you have one. Make a layer of potato slices over the base of a large baking dish or 6 smaller individual baking dishes and season with salt and pepper. Pour over the milk, then add another layer of potato slices, season and sprinkle over half the grated Parmesan. Add a final layer of potato slices, season and pour over the cream, then sprinkle with the remaining Parmesan. Bake for 30 minutes until the potato layers are soft and the top is golden brown.

Meanwhile, heat the olive oil in a saucepan, add the shallot, garlic and shiitake mushrooms and sauté over medium heat until the shallot and garlic are soft but not browned. Add the thyme sprigs and cook until the liquid released by the mushrooms has evaporated. Pour in the white wine and simmer briskly until evaporated. Stir in the tomato purée, chopped tomatoes and sugar, then pour in enough water to cover the mushrooms (about 14 oz/400ml). Season with salt and pepper and all the spices. Simmer for 15–20 minutes until the water has evaporated and the mushrooms are coated in a thick sauce.

RECIPE CONTINUES...

for the béchamel sauce
3½ oz (100 g) butter
3½ oz (100 g) all-purpose flour
4⅓ cups (1 liter) milk
pinch of ground nutmeg
pinch of salt
pinch of white pepper

For the béchamel sauce, melt the butter in a saucepan over medium heat, add the flour and cook, whisking with a balloon whisk, until a smooth paste (roux) forms. Gradually add the milk and cook until the mixture thickens, whisking constantly. Remove the pan from the heat and add the nutmeg, salt and white pepper.

Layer the deep-fried eggplant slices on top of the potato dauphinoise, followed by the mushrooms. Pour in the béchamel sauce and spread over the top of the mushrooms. Sprinkle over the grated Parmesan and bake at the same temperature for 20 minutes until golden brown.

VEGAN MAGIRITSA

Magiritsa is a special soup made from lamb intestines and liver that is served in the early hours of Easter Sunday. According to custom, people attend midnight mass and then return home to eat the soup. We have replaced the intestines and liver with mushrooms to create a delicious vegan alternative. For a non-vegan version, replace the olive oil with the same quantity of butter and finish off the soup with some Avgolemono Sauce (see page 169).

4 oz (125 ml) extra-virgin
   olive oil
1 onion, finely chopped
1 bunch of spring onions,
   chopped
1 lb 2 oz (500 g) chestnut or
   button mushrooms, or
   a mixture, sliced
1 tablespoon cornstarch
8½ cups (2 liters) hot water
1 bunch of dill, chopped
salt and pepper

SERVES 6

Heat the oil in a saucepan, add the onion and spring onions and sauté over medium heat until softened but not browned.

Add the mushrooms to the pan and sauté for a few minutes until softened, then season with a good pinch of salt and generous grinding of pepper. Sprinkle in the cornstarch and stir in the measured hot water. Bring to a boil, stirring constantly, then simmer for about 40 minutes. Add the chopped dill just before removing from the heat. Serve immediately.

Greek cuisine is known for its savory dishes, but there is a sweet side to it that deserves wider attention. It's our mission at MAZI to make Greek desserts known to the world, and we draw inspiration from all over the country.

The key characteristic of Greek desserts is the use of syrup — in fact, there is a whole category of sweet dishes that we call *syropiasta*, which literally means "in syrup." There is an obvious influence from the period when Greece was under the control of the Ottoman Empire, from 1453 to 1821, and similar desserts are to be found in Turkey and throughout the Middle East. You will notice that we use a lot of cinnamon, honey and walnuts in desserts but cream and chocolate less so, which means they are relatively light.

The seasons and traditional celebrations of the year play a major role in terms of when certain desserts or sweet treats are prepared. For example, Semolina Halva (*see* page 238) is eaten on *Kathara Deftera*, or "Clean Monday," the first day of Greek Orthodox Lent before Easter, and during the subsequent seven-week period of fasting, while the brioche-like *tsoureki* (*see* page 243) is reserved for Easter itself. *Melomakarona* (*see* page 220), orange, cinnamon and honey cakes, and *kourabiedes* (*see* page 219), confectioners sugar-coated almond cookies, are customarily enjoyed only at Christmas.

DESSERTS

4½ oz (125 g) filo pastry
2 eggs
3½ oz (100 g) superfine sugar
1 vanilla pod, split lengthways
    and seeds scraped out
2 teaspoons baking powder
grated zest and juice of
    1 orange
4½ oz (125 g) Greek yogurt
3¾ oz (110 ml) sunflower oil
edible flowers, to decorate

for the orange syrup
9 oz (250 g) superfine sugar
5 oz (150 ml) orange juice
7 oz (200 ml) water

for the cardamom custard
18 oz (500 ml) milk
1 teaspoon cardamom seeds
3¾ oz (110 g) superfine sugar
1½ oz (40 g) cornstarch
3 eggs
pinch of salt
1½ oz (40 g) unsalted butter,
    diced

to serve
Kaimaki Ice Cream
    (see page 261)
orange cookies, crumbled

SERVES 5

You won't believe that
these moist and orangey
cakes are made out of
crushed filo pastry! They
are perfect paired with
an aromatic cardamom
custard and a scoop of
traditional Greek kaimaki
ice cream, or Greek Coffee
Ice Cream (see page 263).

PORTOKALOPITA

Unwrap the filo pastry for the cakes and leave to dry out for 5 hours at room temperature.

For the orange syrup, put all the ingredients in a saucepan over medium heat and bring to a boil, stirring until the sugar has dissolved. Continue to boil for 2 minutes until the mixture is slightly syrupy. Remove from the heat and pour into a bowl, then cover and leave to cool in the refrigerator.

Preheat the oven to 475°F (240°C).

Mix the eggs, sugar and vanilla seeds together in a bowl, then mix in the baking powder and orange zest and juice. Fold in the yogurt and then the sunflower oil. Crumble in the filo pastry and mix well, then leave the mixture to rest for 10 minutes in the refrigerator.

Pour the cake mixture into 5 small rectangular/bar-shaped sections of a silicone mold and bake for 13 minutes until golden.

Meanwhile, make the cardamom custard. Add half the milk to a saucepan with the cardamom seeds and heat until it starts to boil, then remove the pan from the heat and leave to infuse for 10 minutes. Strain to remove the cardamom seeds, then return to the pan and whisk in all the remaining ingredients except the butter. Heat over medium heat, whisking constantly, until the mixture thickens. Remove from the heat and beat in the butter, piece by piece, until it is all melted and incorporated. Pour into a bowl, cover the surface with plastic wrap and leave to cool completely.

Remove the silicone mold from the oven. Pour half the cold orange syrup over the cakes and leave to soak in for a few minutes, then repeat with the remaining syrup.

Unmold the cakes and serve them with a little of the cardamom custard. Sit a quenelle (a football-shaped scoop) of the Kaimaki Ice Cream alongside on top of the crumbled orange cookies and decorate with edible flowers.

LOUKOUMADES
WITH LAVENDER HONEY
AND CRUSHED WALNUTS

Loukoumades are the Greek version of doughnuts, and despite being historically regarded as "a poor man's dessert," they have proved to be the most popular sweet dish ever at MAZI. We serve these little deep-fried balls soaked in lavender honey; be warned — once you've eaten one, you'll find it hard to stop! We serve them with Chocolate Sorbet (see page 260) on the side, but Kaimaki Ice Cream goes equally well with them (see page 261).

7 oz (200 ml) milk
7 oz (200 ml) water
1 oz (25 g) superfine sugar
¼ oz (10 g) dried active yeast
12 oz (350 g) all-purpose flour
pinch of salt
2 tablespoons olive oil
shot of ouzo
sunflower oil, for deep-frying

for the lavender honey
7 oz (200 g) honey, or more
    if you like
3 sprigs of dried lavender

to serve
pinch of ground cinnamon
handful of crushed walnuts

SERVES 4

First prepare the lavender honey. Add the honey to a bowl, stir in the lavender sprigs and leave to infuse at room temperature for about an hour.

Put the milk and measured water in a saucepan, stir together and gently warm over medium heat. Put the sugar and yeast in a bowl, then pour in the warm (not hot) milk mixture and stir for a couple of minutes until the mixture becomes foamy.

In a separate large bowl, mix the flour and salt together, then stir in the olive oil and ouzo. Pour in the warm milk and yeast mixture and whisk thoroughly for 2–4 minutes until the mixture is smooth. Cover the bowl with plastic wrap and leave the dough to rest in a warm place for 30 minutes.

Uncover the dough and mix again gently with a flexible spatula. Re-cover and leave to rest in the refrigerator for an hour.

Heat enough sunflower oil for deep-frying in a deep-fryer or a large, deep saucepan to 400°F (200°C). Using your hands, scoop up little balls of dough, then deep-fry in the hot oil, in batches, until golden brown. Drain and place on a plate lined with paper towels to soak up the excess oil.

Serve the *loukoumades* hot with the lavender honey poured over them, sprinkled with the cinnamon and crushed walnuts.

for the quince

1 lb 3 oz (520 g) superfine sugar
18 oz (500 ml) water
1 cinnamon stick
2 lb 4 oz (1 kg) quince, peeled, cored and diced

for the mousse

1 lb 2 oz (500 g) Greek yogurt
grated zest of 1 lemon
1¾ oz (50 g) confectioners sugar
1 vanilla pod, split lengthways and seeds scraped out
10 oz (300 ml) heavy cream

to serve

handful of mixed berries
a few blanched almonds
5 cinnamon cookies, crumbled
edible flowers

SERVES 8–10

Yogurt served with fruit in syrup, often referred to as "spoon sweets," is an all-time classic Greek dessert. Our chosen fruit for the syrup treatment is quince, which features prominently in Greek cuisine, at its best from October to December. And we've turned the traditional accompanying yogurt into a light and airy vanilla and lemon-flavored yogurt mousse.

GREEK YOGURT MOUSSE WITH QUINCE IN SYRUP

The day before you want to serve the dessert, prepare the quince. Put the superfine sugar, measured water and cinnamon stick in a saucepan over medium heat and bring to a boil, stirring until the sugar has dissolved and the mixture is slightly syrupy. Remove from the heat and stir in the diced quince, then pour into a bowl, cover and leave to cool overnight.

The next day, transfer the syrup and quince to a saucepan and simmer for about 10 minutes until the quince is soft and the syrup is thick. Remove from the heat and leave to cool.

Put the yogurt, lemon zest, confectioners sugar and vanilla seeds in a bowl and whisk with a hand-held electric mixer on medium speed. While mixing, pour in the cream in a slow, steady stream and continue whisking until you have a velvety mousse. Cover the bowl with plastic wrap and chill in the refrigerator for 2 hours to set before serving.

Serve the quince over the yogurt mousse, sprinkled with the berries, blanched almonds, crumbled cinnamon cookies and edible flowers.

The mousse will keep in the refrigerator up to 3 days, while the quince in syrup can be stored in an airtight container in the refrigerator and will keep for up to a month.

DIMI'S KOURABIEDES

These little melt-in-the-mouth snowball-like cookies are a traditional festive sweet treat that we serve at MAZI over the Christmas period alongside Melomakarona (see page 220). But since they go perfectly with a cup of tea or coffee, why not enjoy them the rest of the year — store them in a container with a tight-fitting lid and they will last for weeks. Christina's godmother, Dimi, makes the best kourabiedes we have ever tasted, so we stole her recipe and made it our own!

9 oz (250 g) unsalted butter, thoroughly softened but not melted, plus extra for greasing
3½ oz (100 g) blanched almonds
1 lb 2 oz (500 g) all-purpose flour
¼ oz (10 g) baking powder
2 tablespoons confectioners sugar, plus extra for coating and to serve
1 small egg
1 teaspoon vanilla extract

MAKES 70

Grease a frying pan lightly with butter, then heat over medium heat, add the almonds and toast for a few minutes, stirring frequently, until just colored. Leave to cool.

Preheat the oven to 400°F (200°C). Line 2 large baking sheets with parchment paper.

Mix the flour and baking powder together and set aside. Place the remaining ingredients, including the toasted almonds, in a large bowl and mix together well, then add the flour mixture, a cupful at a time so that the dough doesn't become too firm, and knead together with your hands.

Shape the dough into small balls, about the size of a large chocolate truffle, place on the lined baking sheets and bake in batches for 15 minutes or until lightly golden.

Remove the baking sheets from the oven and leave the kourabiedes to cool completely on the baking sheets. Then roll them in confectioners sugar until coated all over. You can sprinkle some extra confectioners sugar over them once arranged on a serving platter to look like they are covered in a fresh fall of snow.

PACKAGE THESE UP NICELY FOR A GREAT CHRISTMAS GIFT.

MELOMAKARONA

We know that the festive season has arrived when the restaurant is filled with the cinnamony scent of these yummy cakes soaked in a honey syrup. They are guaranteed to bring out your festive spirit and make your whole house smell like Christmas.

8½ oz (240 ml) sunflower oil
8½ oz (240 ml) olive oil
2 lb (900 g) all-purpose flour
1½ tablespoons ground
    cinnamon
2 tablespoons baking powder
grated zest of 1 orange
7 oz (200 g) superfine sugar
5½ oz (160 ml) orange juice
1 tablespoon baking soda
crushed walnuts, to serve

for the melomakarona *syrup*
14 oz (400 g) superfine sugar
14 oz (400 ml) water
1 cinammon stick
10½ oz (300 g) honey

MAKES ABOUT 60

Preheat the oven to 410°F (210°C). Line 2 large baking sheets with parchment paper.

Pour the oils into the bowl of a stand mixer fitted with the paddle attachment and mix on slow speed. While the mixer is running, add the flour slowly, followed by the cinnamon, baking powder, orange zest, sugar, orange juice and baking soda. Mix until all the ingredients are well blended.

Using your hands, roll the dough into cylinders about 2 inches (5 cm) long and then flatten them. Place the *melomakarona* on the lined baking sheets and bake for 9–11 minutes until crisp. Remove from the oven and leave them on the baking sheets to cool and firm up.

While the *melomakarona* are cooling, for the syrup, put the sugar, measured water and cinnamon stick in a saucepan over medium heat and bring to a boil, stirring until the sugar has dissolved and the mixture is slightly syrupy, then add the honey and simmer, stirring frequently, for another 10 minutes.

Dip each *melomakarona* in the warm syrup and leave for 5 minutes for the syrup to be absorbed, then return to the lined baking sheets to allow the excess syrup to drip off. To serve, place them on a platter and sprinkle with the crushed walnuts and drizzle with more syrup to decorate. These will keep in an airtight container for up to 2 weeks.

melted butter, for greasing
1 quantity of Melomakarona
   Dough (*see* page 220)
1 quantity of Melomakarona
   Syrup (*see* page 220)
crushed walnuts, to serve

for the chocolate ganache
4½ oz (125 g) dark chocolate,
   broken into pieces
11 oz (320 ml) heavy cream
1 tablespoon Metaxa 5 star
   brandy (or other brandy)

for the hazelnut ice cream
   (optional)
3¾ cups (900 ml) milk
5 oz (140 g) superfine sugar
3½ oz (100 ml) heavy cream
1½ oz (40 g) corn syrup
4¼ oz (120 g) hazelnut paste

**MAKES 1 LARGE TART
(OR 8 OR 10 INDIVIDUAL
TARTS)**

Using the concept of the
original melomakarona
— orange and cinnamon
cakes soaked in a honey
syrup (see page 220) —
as the basis of this tart,
we have created a special
dessert that's perfect
for the festive table.
The hazelnut ice cream
makes a luxurious optional
accompaniment.

MELOMAKARONA TART WITH CHOCOLATE GANACHE

Preheat the oven to 410°F (210°C). Brush a 9¼-inch (23.5 cm) round tart pan (or 8 or 10 individual round tart pans, 3½ inches [9 cm] in diameter) with melted butter.

Follow the method on page 220 to make the *melomakarona* dough. Roll the dough out on a work surface and then use to line your tart pans (or large pan), gently laying the dough in the tins and using your fingertips to press the pastry into the edge and up the side of the pan. Prick the bases with a fork. Scrunch up some parchment paper and place it inside the tart cases to prevent the dough from rising during baking. Bake for 9–11 minutes until crisp.

Meanwhile, for the ganache, melt the chocolate with the cream in a heatproof bowl set over a saucepan of barely simmering water. Remove from the heat, add the brandy and whisk until the mixture is well combined.

At the same time, make the *melomakarona* syrup (page 220).

Remove the *melomakarona* tart crusts from the oven and leave to cool. Dip each tart crust in the syrup and leave for 5 minutes for the syrup to be absorbed, then transfer to parchment paper and allow the excess syrup to drip off. Fill the tart crusts with the chocolate ganache and leave to set in the refrigerator for 1 hour.

Meanwhile, make the hazelnut ice cream if desired. Put the milk and sugar in a saucepan over medium heat and bring to a boil, stirring until the sugar has dissolved. Once the mixture begins to boil, remove from the heat and leave to cool. Put the cream, corn syrup and hazelnut paste in the bowl of a stand mixer fitted with the paddle attachment and beat on medium speed. While the mixer is running, add the cooled milk mixture in a slow, steady stream and mix until well blended.

Transfer the mixture to a bowl, cover and leave to cool in the refrigerator, then churn in an ice cream machine for 40 minutes. Store in a freezerproof container in the freezer for up to 2 months.

To serve, sprinkle the ganache with crushed walnuts and serve with scoops of the hazelnut ice cream, if you have made it.

SWEET BOUGATSA WITH HOMEMADE "MILKO"

A northern Greece speciality, bougatsa can be either savory, made with creamy feta cheese, or sweet, made with custard, cinnamon and confectioners sugar, typically eaten in the morning with a side of chocolate milk. Milko is the most popular brand of chocolate milk, so much so that people now call any chocolate milk "Milko." There are stores in Greece entirely devoted to serving bougatsa, called bougatsatzidika, that open from 4am until lunchtime, and you will often see people lining up outside in the very early hours, some for their hangover cure and others for an early breakfast before going to work. And that's why bougatsa features on our Sunday brunch menu.

for the chocolate milk
3⅓ cups (800 ml) milk
1¾ oz (50 g) cocoa powder
1 oz (30 g) honey
2¼ oz (60 g) superfine sugar

for the pastry cream
4⅓ cups (1 liter) milk
10½ oz (300 g) superfine sugar
8 egg yolks
2¼ oz (60 g) fine semolina
2¼ oz (60 g) cornstarch
1 vanilla pod, split lengthways
   and seeds scraped out, or
   1–2 teaspoons vanilla extract
grated zest of 1 lemon
grated zest of 1 orange

for the filo
1 lb 2 oz (500 g) filo pastry
7 oz (200 g) butter, melted

to serve
confectioners sugar
ground cinnamon

SERVES 8

First make the chocolate milk. Put the milk and cocoa powder in a saucepan over medium heat and bring to a simmer, stirring. Add the honey and sugar and continue to heat, stirring constantly, until they have dissolved. Remove from the heat and leave to cool. Then pour into a clean bottle and chill in the refrigerator until ready to serve.

For the pastry cream, put the milk and half the sugar in a saucepan over a medium heat and bring to a boil, stirring until the sugar has dissolved.

Meanwhile, using a balloon whisk, whisk the egg yolks with the remaining sugar in a heatproof bowl until well combined, then whisk in the semolina and cornstarch until smooth. Add the vanilla and citrus zest and whisk again.

While whisking constantly, add the hot milk mixture to the egg yolk mixture in a slow, steady stream until well blended. Then pour the mixture back into the saucepan over medium heat and whisk constantly until the mixture thickens and starts to bubble. Remove from the heat and set aside.

Preheat the oven to 475°F (240°C).

Lay 3 filo pastry sheets, one on top of the other, in the base of a large shallow cake pan, about 14 x 16 inches (35 x 40 cm), brushing each with melted butter as you stack them. Pour in the pastry cream and spread it out in an even layer. Cover with another 3 filo pastry sheets, again brushing each with melted butter. Fold in the overhanging filo around the edges of the cake pan, making sure there are no holes, to make it look like a sealed parcel. Brush the top well with butter and bake for 15–17 minutes until golden.

Remove the bougatsa from the oven and cut the parcel into small squarish portions. Sprinkle with lots of confectioners sugar and cinnamon and serve hot with a glass of the cold chocolate milk.

GALAKTOBOUREKO

6 oz (175 g) butter, plus extra, melted, for brushing the filo
4½ oz (125 g) fine semolina
3 cups (750 ml) milk
5½ oz (150 g) superfine sugar
1 vanilla pod, split lengthways and the seeds scraped out
grated zest of ½ lemon
1 × 8 oz (250 g) pack of filo pastry (12 sheets)
5 egg yolks

for the syrup
10 oz (300 ml) water
1 lb 4 oz (550 g) superfine sugar
½ vanilla pod
2 pinches of ground cinnamon
juice of ½ lemon
1 oz (30 g) corn syrup
1¾ oz (50 g) honey

to serve (optional)
vanilla ice cream
chocolate tuiles

MAKES 6

Kate Lough of the London Evening Standard described this dessert: "It's kind of like a millefeuille, but the vanilla custard center is baked with, not after, the layers upon layers of filo pastry. Doused in sweet syrup, this is the nicest pudding I have ever eaten in London. I could have eaten three." Enough said.
   To form the filo pouches, you will need a clean bottle about 5–5½ inches (13–14 cm) tall and six small round metal pastry rings about 3¼ inches (8 cm) in diameter.

Melt the butter in a saucepan over medium heat and stir in the semolina. Add the milk, sugar, vanilla seeds and lemon zest and continue to heat, stirring constantly, until the mixture thickens. Transfer to a bowl, cover the surface with plastic wrap and leave to cool completely.

Meanwhile, for the syrup, put all the ingredients, except the honey, in a saucepan over medium heat and bring to a boil, stirring until the sugar has dissolved. Continue to boil for 5–8 minutes until the mixture is syrupy. Remove from the heat, add the honey and stir until dissolved and well blended. Remove from the heat and pour into a bowl, then cover and leave to cool in the refrigerator.

Preheat the oven to 475°F (240°C). Line a baking sheet with parchment paper.

Lay a sheet of filo pastry horizontally on a work surface. Brush with melted butter and place a second sheet of filo vertically on top. Brush the second sheet with melted butter, then place a third filo sheet on top horizontally and brush it with butter. Stand your small clean bottle in the center of the filo sheets and fold them up around it to form a pouch. Brush one of your small round pastry rings with butter and slip over the pastry-encased bottle, then remove the bottle, keeping the cutter in place, and fill the pouch with the custard. Fold the top of the pouch over to seal, making sure there are no holes. Brush the outside with butter. Repeat with the remaining filo pastry and custard to make another 5 pouches.

Place the galaktobourekos on the lined baking sheet and bake for 15–18 minutes until golden.

To serve, carefully remove the pastry ring from each galaktoboureko. Top with scoops of vanilla ice cream and decorate with chocolate tuiles, if liked. Remove the vanilla pod from the cold syrup, then pour the syrup over the hot galaktobourekos.

for the caramelized nuts

7 oz (200 g) superfine sugar

7 oz (200 g) whole blanched
   hazelnuts

7 oz (200 g) whole blanched
   almonds

for the syrup

2 lb 4 oz (1 kg) superfine sugar

20 oz (600 ml) water

7 oz (200 g) corn syrup

juice of 1 lemon

for the almond custard

4⅓ cups (1 liter) milk

7 oz (200 g) butter

9 oz (250 g) superfine sugar

5 eggs

3 oz (80 g) cornstarch

scant ½ teaspoon (2 ml) almond
   extract

for the kataifi

2 lb 4 oz (1 kg) kataifi pastry

9 oz (250 g) butter

to serve (optional)

chocolate sauce (*see* page 237)

fresh mixed berries

SERVES 8

Inspired by the traditional
Greek dessert ekmek kataifi
made with kataifi (shredded
filo) pastry (available in
Greek and Middle Eastern
delis, online and in larger
supermarkets), which
resembles tousled angel's
hair, topped with custard and
whipped cream, our version
has an almond custard and
caramelized nuts.

ANGEL HAIR WITH ALMOND CUSTARD AND CARAMELIZED NUTS

For the caramelized nuts, heat a heavy-based saucepan over medium heat. Add half the sugar in an even layer and heat over medium heat, without stirring, until it starts to melt at the edges. Swirl the pan to distribute the melted sugar around the pan so that it doesn't burn and to help the rest melt, then continue to heat until all the sugar has caramelized. Then immediately add the remaining sugar and swirl the pan to distribute the melted sugar as before. Continue to heat until all the sugar has caramelized. As soon as the caramel is ready, add the nuts and toss them around until well coated. Transfer to a sheet of parchment paper and leave to cool.

For the syrup, put all the ingredients in a saucepan over medium heat and bring to a boil, stirring until the sugar has dissolved and the mixture is slightly syrupy. Remove from the heat and pour into a bowl, then cover and leave to cool in the refrigerator.

For the custard, put the milk and butter in a saucepan over medium heat and bring to a boil, stirring until the butter has melted. As the mixture is heating, using a balloon whisk, whisk the sugar and eggs together in a heatproof bowl until well combined, then whisk in the cornstarch and almond extract until smooth. While whisking constantly, add the hot milk mixture in a slow, steady stream until well blended. Then pour the mixture into a clean saucepan and heat gently, whisking constantly, until the mixture thickens. Remove from the heat, cover the surface with plastic wrap and leave to cool. The custard can be used at room temperature or made in advance and kept in the refrigerator.

Preheat the oven to 400°F (200°C).

For the kataifi, separate the strands of kataifi pastry and spread them over a baking sheet in an even layer. Heat the butter in a saucepan and, once melted, pour over the kataifi. Bake for 18–20 minutes until golden brown.

To serve, cut the pastry into 8 evenly sized rectangular pieces. Decorate each plate with a smear of chocolate sauce, if liked, and then top with a pastry rectangle. Pipe the almond custard on top and sprinkle with the caramelized nuts, fresh mixed berries and any surplus pastry strands.

AMYGDALOPITA

This almond cake is not only delicious but also gluten free. Try serving it with a scoop of Kaimaki Ice Cream on the side (see page 261).

7 oz (200 g) butter, softened, plus extra for greasing
1 lb 2 oz (500 g) superfine sugar, plus extra for sprinkling
7 oz (200 ml) olive oil
1 lb 2 oz (500 g) ground almonds
7 eggs
grated zest of 1 lemon
grated zest of 1 small orange
2¼ oz (60 g) cornstarch
handful of flaked almonds

for the pastry cream
4⅓ cups (1 liter) milk
7 oz (200 g) superfine sugar
1 vanilla pod, split lengthways and seeds scraped out
6 egg yolks
1¾ oz (50 g) cornstarch

SERVES 12

First make the pastry cream. Put the milk, half the sugar and the vanilla seeds in a saucepan over medium heat and bring to a boil, stirring until the sugar has dissolved.

Meanwhile, using a balloon whisk, whisk the egg yolks with the remaining sugar in a heatproof bowl until well combined, then whisk in the cornstarch.

While whisking constantly, add most of the hot milk mixture to the egg yolk mixture in a slow, steady stream until well blended. Then pour the mixture back into the saucepan over medium heat and whisk constantly until the mixture thickens and starts to bubble. Remove from the heat, then pour into a bowl, cover the surface with plastic wrap and leave to cool completely.

Grease a large shallow cake pan, about 14 x 16 inches (35 x 40cm), with butter.

Put the butter and sugar in the bowl of a stand mixer fitted with the paddle attachment and beat on medium speed until pale and fluffy. Add the olive oil and ground almonds and beat in, then beat in the eggs, one by one. Finally, add the citrus zest, cornstarch and pastry cream and fold in gently.

Add the cake mixture to the greased cake pan and chill in the refrigerator for 30 minutes. Meanwhile, preheat the oven to 375°F (190°C).

Sprinkle the top of the cake with the flaked almonds and some superfine sugar and bake for 40–50 minutes until the cake is golden brown and a skewer inserted into the center of the cake comes out clean.

Remove the cake from the oven and leave to cool in the pan for a few minutes. Then remove the cake from the pan and transfer to a wire rack to cool completely. It will keep for 4–5 days.

4½ oz (125 g) butter, softened,
  plus extra for greasing
11½ oz (330 g) all-purpose flour
11½ oz (330 g) walnuts, crushed,
  plus an extra handful of
  crushed walnuts to decorate
1 oz (25 g) baking powder
1 teaspoon ground cinnamon
1 teaspoon ground cloves
7¾ oz (220 g) superfine sugar
3 eggs
4 oz (125 ml) milk
shot of Metaxa 5 star brandy
  (or other brandy)

for the syrup
1 lb 4 oz (550 g) superfine sugar
15½ oz (440 ml) water

**for the chocolate sauce
  (optional)**
1 lb 2 oz (500 g) dark chocolate,
  broken into pieces
18 oz (500 ml) heavy cream

SERVES 8–10

WALNUT AND
METAXA CAKE

First make the syrup. Put the sugar and measured water in a saucepan over medium heat and bring to a boil, stirring until the sugar has dissolved. Continue to boil for 5–8 minutes until the mixture is syrupy. Remove from the heat and pour into a bowl, then cover and leave to cool in the refrigerator.

Preheat the oven to 375°F (190°C). Grease a 12-inch (30 cm) square cake pan with butter.

Put the flour, walnuts, baking powder, cinnamon and cloves into a bowl and mix together well.

Put the butter and sugar in the bowl of a stand mixer fitted with the paddle attachment and beat on medium speed until pale and fluffy. Beat in the eggs, one by one, followed by the milk and brandy. Reduce the speed, add the dry mixture and mix until well incorporated. Pour the cake mixture into the greased cake pan and bake for 40–45 minutes until golden brown.

Remove the cake from the oven, then pour the cold syrup all over the cake and leave to soak in for a few minutes. Finally, sprinkle over the handful of crushed walnuts.

For the chocolate sauce, if using, put the chocolate in a saucepan with the cream and heat gently, stirring, until melted and well combined. Pour over individual slices of the cake and serve immediately.

This recipe is inspired by the Greek classic karydopita, a moist walnut cake flavored with ground cinnamon and cloves and soaked in syrup. We have added Metaxa brandy to the cake mixture and then poured an optional dark chocolate sauce all over it to make it even more indulgent and mouthwatering.

SEMOLINA HALVA

This vegan dessert is considered by Greeks to be the "healthy" sweet option and is mostly eaten during Lent when dairy products are out of bounds.

1 lb 9 oz (700 g) superfine sugar
4⅓ cups (1 liter) water
9 oz (250 ml) olive oil, plus extra for oiling
1 lb ½ oz (460 g) coarse semolina
½ teaspoon ground cinnamon, plus extra for sprinkling
½ teaspoon ground cloves
grated zest of 1 orange
5½ oz (150 g) mixed unsalted nuts, crushed

SERVES 6

Put the sugar and measured water in a saucepan over medium heat and bring to a boil, stirring until the sugar has dissolved. Continue to boil until the mixture is syrupy.

Meanwhile, lightly brush a nonstick bundt cake pan with olive oil.

In a separate saucepan, heat the olive oil over medium heat and stir in the semolina. Reduce the heat and cook, stirring constantly, for 5–8 minutes until the semolina browns.

Pour in the syrup, add the cinnamon, cloves, orange zest and crushed nuts and continue cooking over low heat, stirring, for 5–8 minutes until the mixture becomes firm.

Remove the pan from the heat and pour the mixture into the prepared mold. Cover with plastic wrap and chill in the refrigerator for 2–3 hours until completely firm.

To serve, unmold the pudding on to a plate, sprinkle with cinnamon and cut into slices.

WARM RICE PUDDING WITH VANILLA AND LEMON

Called rizogalo in Greek, which literally translates to "rice milk," this humble dessert flavored with vanilla seeds and lemon rind is creamy and comforting.

5½ oz (150 g) Arborio rice
7 oz (200 g) superfine sugar
22 oz (625 ml) milk
18½ oz (525 ml) heavy cream
pared rind of 1 lemon
1 vanilla pod, split lengthways
    and seeds scraped out
1¾ oz (50 g) cornstarch
pinch of ground cinnamon,
    to serve

SERVES 8

Cook the rice in a saucepan of boiling water for 5 minutes.

Drain the rice and return it to the pan with the sugar, milk, cream, lemon rind and vanilla seeds. Simmer very gently for 40–50 minutes or until relatively thick, stirring frequently so the mixture doesn't stick to the base of the pan or boil for too long.

Remove the lemon rind. Mix the cornstarch with a little cold water to make a smooth paste, then stir into the rice mixture and cook gently, stirring, for a few more minutes until thickened.

Remove from the heat and immediately pour the rice pudding into individual bowls, then sprinkle each with cinnamon before serving.

THIS IS
EQUALLY GOOD
SERVED COLD.

MASTIHA RAVANI

Ravani is a delicious semolina cake that is guaranteed to make you drool and then beg for more. It comes in different flavors, including coconut and lemon, but our version features the distinctively aromatic mastiha, a key Greek ingredient that comes from the resin of the mastiha (or mastic) tree, cultivated on the island of Chios, with a protected designation of origin (PDO) status. Mastiha has been widely valued for its therapeutic qualities since ancient times and more recently for a variety of uses in different forms including powder and crystals for flavoring cakes (as here), ice creams and other desserts, a gum (often called gum mastic) for making chewing gum and as a sweet, clear liqueur (see page 14) and a body oil.

The crystals are available from the same sources as the powder — Greek and Middle Eastern delis or food stores or from online specialist ingredient suppliers.

butter, for greasing
6 eggs, separated
5 oz (140 g) superfine sugar
5 oz (140 g) coarse semolina
2½ oz (70 g) all-purpose flour
pinch of mastiha powder

for the syrup
10½ oz (300 g) superfine sugar
10 oz (300 ml) water
1 lemon, halved
⅛ oz (5 g) mastiha crystals

SERVES 8

Preheat the oven to 375°F (190°C). Grease a rectangular cake pan about 12¾ x 8½ inches (32 x 22 cm), and 2 inches (5 cm) deep, with butter.

Put the egg yolks and 3¼ oz (90 g) of the sugar in the bowl of a stand mixer fitted with the whisk attachment and whisk on medium speed until pale and fluffy.

In a separate large, grease-free bowl, using a hand-held electric mixer on medium speed, beat the egg whites until stiff peaks form. Increase the speed and mix in the remaining 1¾ oz (50 g) sugar, a spoonful at a time, mixing well between additions, until the mixture is thick and glossy.

Add half the meringue mixture to the egg yolk mixture and fold in gently, followed by the semolina, flour, mastiha powder and the rest of the meringue, again folding in gently.

Add the mixture to the greased cake pan and bake for 20–25 minutes until golden and a skewer inserted into the center of the cake comes out clean. Remove the cake from the oven and leave to cool completely in the pan.

Meanwhile, make the syrup. Put all the ingredients in a saucepan over medium heat and bring to a boil, stirring until the sugar and mastiha have dissolved. Continue to boil for a few minutes until the mixture is slightly syrupy.

Pour the hot syrup on to the cooled cake and leave to soak in for several minutes before serving. Any left over will keep for up to 3 days.

EASTER TSOUREKI

Tsoureki is a sort of braided brioche that historically Greek women would bake on the Thursday before Easter ready to eat from Easter Day onwards. Although still largely associated with Easter, tsoureki is too good not to enjoy all year round. Try it topped with chocolate hazelnut spread and dipped into a glass of milk or cup of coffee — glorious!

Red-dyed eggs are a traditional Greek Easter custom. They are used as table decorations on Easter Sunday or baked into this traditional Greek Easter bread. Symbolic of resurrection and new life, the eggs are also cracked on Easter Sunday as part of the fun game tsougrisma.

Mahlepi or mahlab powder is the ground seed from the stones of St. Lucie or mahaleb cherries, which has a bitter almond/cherry-like flavor. You can buy it from Greek and Middle Eastern delis or food stores or from online specialist ingredient suppliers.

1 lb 9 oz (700 g) bread flour
6¼ oz (180 g) superfine sugar
pinch of salt
2 eggs, plus 1 for glazing
9 oz (250 ml) milk
1¾ oz (50 g) fast-action dried yeast
4½ oz (130 g) unsalted butter, softened and diced
1 teaspoon mahlepi (mahlab) powder
sprinkling of flaked almonds

MAKES 2 MEDIUM TSOUREKI

Put the flour, sugar, salt, 2 eggs, milk and yeast in a large bowl and knead together with your hands until well blended. Add the butter, piece by piece, and knead in, then continue kneading until the dough is soft and elastic — how long this takes will vary, so you can only judge by the feel of the dough. Finally, add the mahlepi powder and knead the dough until well incorporated.

Form the dough into a round ball and place in a large plastic bowl, ideally, or other large bowl. Cover with a clean kitchen towel or plastic wrap and leave the dough to rest in a warm place for 2–3 hours until it doubles in size.

Line a large baking sheet with parchment paper. Knead the dough briefly on a work surface to deflate it, then divide into 6 pieces and roll each into a rope. For each tsoureki, press the ends of 3 ropes together, then braid the free ends and press the other ends together. Place the tsoureki on the lined baking sheet, cover as before and leave to rest in a warm place for a further hour.

Meanwhile, preheat the oven to 375°F (190°C).

Beat the remaining egg with a little water, brush the tsoureki gently to glaze and sprinkle with flaked almonds. Bake for about 40 minutes until golden brown. Remove from the oven and leave to cool. The tsoureki will keep, well wrapped at room temperature, for up to a week.

TSOUREKI FONDANT WITH GREEK COFFEE ICE CREAM

This pudding tastes just like the traditional Easter sweet bread tsoureki, with the distinctive bitter almond/cherry flavoring of mahlepi (mahlab) powder (see page 243) along with a hint of aromatic mastiha powder (see page 14), both available from Greek and Middle Eastern delis or food stores or online. This was for many years one of our most famous desserts and it still makes a comeback every Easter Day at MAZI. Serving it with Greek Coffee Ice Cream (see page 263) on the side is another reference to tsoureki, which is customarily dipped into Greek coffee before eating.

3½ oz (100 g) butter, diced, plus extra for greasing

4½ oz (130 g) superfine sugar, plus extra for sprinkling

9 oz (250 g) white chocolate chips

5 eggs

⅓ oz (12 g) mahlepi (mahlab) powder

⅛ oz (5 g) mastiha powder

¼ oz (10 g) black sesame seeds

5½ oz (150 g) all-purpose flour, sifted

confectioners sugar, for sprinkling

Greek Coffee Ice Cream (see page 263), to serve

MAKES 6

Preheat the oven to 425°F (220°C). Grease 6 individual ramekins with butter and sprinkle with superfine sugar until well coated. Transfer to a baking sheet.

Melt the white chocolate and butter in a heatproof bowl set over a pan of barely simmering water. Remove from the heat and stir until combined and smooth.

Put the superfine sugar, eggs, mahlepi powder, mastiha powder and sesame seeds in the bowl of a stand mixer fitted with the whisk attachment and whisk on medium speed until thick and pale. Add the melted chocolate mixture and mix in, then fold in the flour, a small amount at a time, until well combined.

Pour the mixture into the prepared ramekins until half-filled and bake for 8 minutes until golden. (Don't be tempted to bake these for more than 8 minutes as they will lose their fondant centers.)

Remove from the oven, sprinkle with confectioners sugar and serve immediately with a scoop of Greek Coffee Ice Cream on the side.

MAMA'S BRAIDED COOKIES

Stocking up on homemade cookies is a must in any Greek household — essential for when a neighbor should come around unannounced for a "quick" coffee. At MAZI, we bake these cookies on a constant basis to serve with our Greek coffee.

Although this recipe makes a large quantity, the cookies are very light and airy — six people ate a whole batch over two days at the photoshoot — and easy to make. But you can easily halve the recipe if you want to make a smaller quantity.

1 lb 2 oz (500 g) unsalted butter, softened
13 oz (375 g) superfine sugar
2 eggs
1 teaspoon vanilla extract
1 lb 2 oz (500 g) all-purpose flour, plus an extra 2½ oz (70 g) if needed

MAKES ABOUT 120

Preheat the oven to 400°F (200°C). Line 4 large baking sheets with parchment paper.

Put the butter and sugar in the bowl of a stand mixer fitted with the paddle attachment and mix on medium speed until pale and fluffy. Beat in the eggs and vanilla extract until well blended. Then add the flour, a small amount at a time, and mix until well incorporated, adding the extra if needed, until the dough no longer sticks to the side of the bowl.

To make the cookies, take a small piece of dough and roll it into a 1-inch (2.5 cm) ball and then roll this out to a length approximately 6 inches (15 cm) long. For each cookie, fold the length in half then twist 2 times to form a twisted braid. Place the cookies on the lined baking sheets and bake in batches for about 12 minutes until golden.

Remove the baking sheets from the oven and leave the cookies to cool completely on the sheets. Store in an airtight container — they should keep well for up to 1 month.

DATE AND MERINGUE TOURTA

We are fortunate to have been given this recipe by Aspa, a legendary lady of Thessaloniki whose family has owned one of the best pâtisseries in town since 1938, called Ellinikon. It is one of their signature desserts and has been the star turn at a multitude of dinner parties and afternoon teas through the decades.

melted butter, for greasing
9 oz (250 g) dried dates, pitted and roughly chopped, plus a few whole dates to decorate
9 oz (250 g) walnuts, roughly chopped, plus a few whole walnuts to decorate
2 tablespoons all-purpose flour
10 egg whites
scant 1 teaspoon cream of tartar
8½ oz (240 g) superfine sugar
14 oz (400 ml) heavy cream
½ vanilla pod, split lengthways and seeds scraped out, or 1 teaspoon of vanilla extract

SERVES 8

Preheat the oven to, ideally, 385°F (195°C), or 400°F (200°C). Brush a springform cake pan about 10 inches (25 cm) in diameter with butter and line the base with parchment paper.

Mix the chopped dates and walnuts and the flour together in a bowl.

Put the egg whites and cream of tartar in the bowl of a stand mixer fitted with the whisk attachment and whisk on medium speed, or beat with a hand-held electric mixer in a large, grease-free bowl, until stiff peaks form. Increase the speed and whisk in the sugar, a spoonful at a time, whisking well between additions, until the mixture is thick and glossy. Gently fold in the date and walnut mixture.

Add the mixture to the prepared pan and bake for 45 minutes until firm to the touch. Remove from the oven and leave to cool in the pan for 5–10 minutes. Then release the cake from the pan, transfer to a serving platter and leave to cool completely.

Whip the cream with the vanilla seeds or extract in a bowl until thick. Spread some of the vanilla cream around the sides of the meringue and then pipe the remainder on top of the cake and onto the plate around it. Decorate with the whole dates and walnuts.

KOLOKITHOPITA

The recipe for this sweet, cinnamon-spiced butternut squash filo pastry pie comes from Christina's grandmother, who would make it faithfully every year on Christmas Day.

3½ oz (100 ml) olive oil
1 small onion, grated
1 butternut squash, peeled, deseeded and grated
5 tablespoons superfine sugar, plus extra if needed to taste
1 heaped tablespoon ground cinnamon
1 lb 2 oz (500 g) filo pastry
handful of cloves, to decorate

for the syrup
1 lb 5 oz (600 g) superfine sugar
19¾ oz (590 ml) water

SERVES 6

Preheat the oven to 400°F (200°C).

Heat a drizzle of the olive oil in a saucepan, add the onion and sauté over medium heat for 5 minutes, stirring, until soft. Add the squash and sugar and sauté until the squash is soft. Continue cooking until all the liquid has evaporated, then finally add the cinnamon and stir well. Check the sweetness, as you may need to add a little more sugar. Remove from the heat and set aside.

Lay a sheet of filo pastry vertically on a work surface and brush half of it with olive oil. Fold the other half on top and brush the top with olive oil. Place 2–3 tablespoons of the filling across the center of the folded filo, then roll up into a cylinder. Place on a large round baking sheet. Continue with the remaining filo pastry sheets, arranging the cylinders on the sheet end to end in a curve to form a spiral.

When the whole sheet has been covered, brush the top of the spiral with olive oil and scatter the cloves over it. Bake for 40–50 minutes until golden brown.

Meanwhile, make the syrup. Put the sugar and measured water in a saucepan over medium heat and bring to a boil, stirring until the sugar has dissolved. Continue to boil for about 5 minutes until the mixture is syrupy.

Remove the pie from the oven, then pour over the hot syrup and serve.

7 oz (200 g) butter, melted, plus
   extra for greasing if needed
2 × 8 oz (250 g) packs of filo
   pastry (24 sheets)

for the pastry cream
3½ oz (100 g) all-purpose flour
1¾ oz (50 g) cornstarch
12 oz (350 g) superfine sugar
4⅓ cups (1 liter) whole milk
2 eggs, beaten
3½ oz (100 g) butter, diced
1 vanilla pod

for the syrup
1 lb 2 oz (500 g) superfine sugar
14 oz (400 ml) water
a few drops of lemon juice

MAKES 24

Panorama is an upmarket
suburb of Thessaloniki
where local pâtisseries
specialize in these
renowned pastry triangles,
trigona, filled with cream.
The trigona Panoramatos
was once just a local
speciality, yet the word
has spread and it is now
a much-loved dessert
throughout Greece.

TRIGONA PANORAMATOS

For the pastry cream, mix together the flour, cornstarch and sugar in a large bowl. Put the milk and beaten eggs in a saucepan over medium heat. Add the dry ingredients from the bowl and bring the mixture to a boil, stirring constantly, until the sugar is dissolved and the mixture thickens and starts to bubble. Immediately remove from the heat and add the butter and vanilla pod, continuing to stir until well combined. Return to the bowl, cover the surface with plastic wrap and leave to cool completely.

Preheat the oven to 350°F (180°C). Line 2 baking sheets with silicone baking mats, or use parchment paper and grease with butter.

Lay a sheet of filo pastry vertically on a work surface, then cut it into 3 vertical strips. Take the first strip and brush it with melted butter, then place a second strip on top and again brush with butter. Repeat with the third strip. Fold one corner of the triple-layered filo strip over to meet the opposite side to form a triangle and then continue folding the triangle over on itself to reach the end of the strip. Cut the triangle in half into 2 smaller triangles. Open the triangles out to make cones and place some scrunched-up parchment paper in each cone to keep their shape. Place the cones on one of the prepared baking sheets. Repeat with the remaining filo pastry sheets. Brush the cones with melted butter and bake for 30 minutes until golden.

While the cones are baking, prepare the syrup. Put all the ingredients in a saucepan over medium heat and bring to a boil, stirring until the sugar has dissolved. Continue to boil for 5–8 minutes until the mixture is syrupy. Remove from the heat and leave to cool.

Remove the cones from the oven and remove the parchment paper from inside. Immediately dip the cones, one by one, into the syrup, leaving them in the syrup for a few seconds, then remove and place on a serving platter. Remove the vanilla pod from the pastry cream and then spoon the cream into a piping bag and pipe it into the cones. Serve immediately or store in the refrigerator to serve later — they will keep for 3–4 days.

ARMENOVIL

A speciality of Thessaloniki, armenovil is a gorgeous semifreddo dessert with caramelized almonds and crushed meringues, over which a hot dark chocolate sauce is poured just before serving. Given what an amazing dish this is, it was surprising to discover that it is relatively unknown in Greece outside of Thessaloniki, as it was to many of our chefs at MAZI.

3 egg whites
¼ teaspoon cream of tartar
   or ½ teaspoon lemon juice
6¼ oz (180 g) superfine sugar
¼ teaspoon vanilla extract
butter, for greasing
17 oz (480 ml) heavy cream
4 egg yolks

for the caramelized nuts
5½ oz (150 g) superfine sugar
5½ oz (150 g) whole blanched
   almonds, crushed

for the chocolate sauce
7 oz (200 g) dark chocolate,
   broken into pieces
3½ oz (100 g) butter, diced

SERVES 10

Preheat the oven to 265°F (130°C).

First make the meringues. Put the egg whites and cream of tartar or lemon juice in the bowl of a stand mixer fitted with the whisk attachment and whisk on medium speed until stiff peaks form. Increase the speed and whisk in the sugar, a spoonful at a time, whisking well between additions, and then the vanilla extract, until the mixture is thick and glossy.

Line a baking sheet with parchment paper and grease it with butter. Place the meringue mixture in a piping bag fitted with a medium star piping nozzle and pipe small rosettes on to the greased parchment paper. Bake for about 2 hours or until dry.

Meanwhile, follow the method on page 230 to prepare the caramelized nuts.

When the meringues are ready, remove from the oven and leave to cool on the baking sheet, then crush.

Add the cream and egg yolks to the cleaned bowl of your stand mixer fitted with the paddle attachment and beat on high speed until thick. Add two-thirds of the caramelized nuts and then the crushed meringues and mix together.

Tip the mixture into a deep round mold or cake pan about 4 inch (20 cm) in diameter and 3¼ inches (8 cm) deep, or a long rectangular mold or cake pan about 12 x 3½ inches (30 x 9 cm) and 2¾ inches (7 cm) deep. Cover with plastic wrap and place in the freezer for at least 24 hours before serving. (You can store it in the freezer for up to 2 weeks.)

When you are ready to serve, melt the chocolate with the butter in a heatproof bowl set over a pan of barely simmering water. Unmold the *armenovil* by dipping the base of the mold briefly in hot water and turning it out on to a serving platter. Pour the hot chocolate sauce over the top and serve immediately decorated with the remaining caramelized nuts.

PISTACHIO AND MASTIHA PARFAIT

Parfait is an old-school frozen creamy dessert similar to ice cream but light and very refreshing. It makes the perfect ending to a substantial meal, winter or summer. We serve it with our Green Apple Sorbet on the side (see page 260), seated on a bed of crushed pistachio nuts.

12 egg yolks
5½ oz (150 g) green pistachio
    paste
9 oz (250 ml) heavy cream
2¼ oz (60 g) superfine sugar
2 shots of mastiha liqueur
juice of 1 lemon
Green Apple Sorbet
    (see page 260), to serve

for the syrup
5½ oz (150 g) superfine sugar
4 tablespoons (60 ml) water

to decorate
crushed pistachio nuts
edible flowers

SERVES 10

First make the syrup. Put the sugar and measured water in a saucepan and heat gently, stirring, until the sugar has dissolved, then simmer until the mixture is syrupy.

Put the egg yolks in the bowl of a stand mixer fitted with the whisk attachment and whisk on high speed until creamy. While the mixer is running, add the hot syrup in a slow, steady stream, followed by the green pistachio paste.

Whisk the cream, sugar and mastiha liqueur together in a separate bowl until thick and creamy. Slowly fold this mixture into the egg yolk and pistachio mixture, then fold in the lemon juice.

Pour the mixture into 10 small round or rectangular/bar-shaped sections of a silicone mold and place in the freezer for a minimum of 2 hours until they are set. Unmould to serve alongside a ball of Green Apple Sorbet seated on a bed of crushed pistachio nuts. Decorate with edible flowers.

GREEN APPLE SORBET

Fruity, refreshing and sharp, we created this sorbet specially to go with our Pistachio and Mastiha Parfait (see page 259). But equally, feel free to enjoy the sorbet on its own.

3⅓ cups (800 ml) water
14 oz (400 g) superfine sugar
8½ oz (240 g) corn syrup
1 lb 2 oz (500 g) green dessert
   apples (like Granny Smith),
   grated

SERVES 10

Put the measured water, sugar and corn syrup in a saucepan and bring to a boil, stirring until the sugar has dissolved. Continue to boil for about 5 minutes, stirring, until the mixture thickens. Remove from the heat and leave to cool.

Add the syrup to a food processor or blender with the grated apples and blend until smooth, then pass through a fine-mesh strainer.

Transfer the mixture to an ice cream machine and churn for 40 minutes. Store in a freezerproof container in the freezer for up to 2 months.

CHOCOLATE SORBET

This has a full, dark chocolate taste without the addition of cream or milk. So as well as being truly scrumptious, you can enjoy it (relatively) free of guilt. Serve on its own or with our Loukoumades (see page 214) as we do at the restaurant.

13 oz (375 ml) water
7 oz (200 g) superfine sugar
2¾ oz (75 g) cocoa powder
6¼ oz (180 g) dark chocolate
   chips
6¼ oz (180 g) ice cubes

SERVES 6

Put the measured water, sugar and cocoa powder in a saucepan over medium heat and bring to a simmer, stirring, and continue to simmer for 10 minutes.

Meanwhile, melt the chocolate chips in a heatproof bowl set over a pan of barely simmering water.

Pour the cocoa mixture into a separate bowl, add the melted chocolate chips and then the ice cubes and whisk together well.

Transfer the mixture to an ice cream machine and churn for 40 minutes. Store in a freezerproof container in the freezer for up to 2 months.

KAIMAKI ICE CREAM

Kaimaki or dondurma ice cream is the original ice cream of Greece, its recipe influenced by the culinary traditions of the ruling Ottoman Empire. Its unique taste comes from sahlep powder, the dried and ground tubers of wild orchids, and mastiha powder, made from the resin of the mastiha tree (see page 241), both available from Greek and Middle Eastern delis or food stores or from online specialist ingredient suppliers. Traditionally, buffalo milk is used, but cow milk will do just fine. This ice cream goes very well with our Portokalopita (see page 212) or Amygdalopita (see page 233) cakes.

4⅓ cups (1 liter) milk
7¾ oz (220 ml) heavy cream
9 oz (250 g) superfine sugar
3½ oz (100 g) corn syrup
⅛ oz (5 g) sahlep powder
scant ⅛ oz (4 g) mastiha
    powder
1 cinnamon stick

SERVES 8–10

Put all the ingredients in a saucepan over medium heat and bring to a simmer, stirring until the sugar has dissolved. Add a sugar thermometer to the pan and continue to heat until the mixture reaches 167°F (75°C) on the thermometer.

Remove from the heat and leave the mixture to cool, then pass through a fine-mesh strainer twice.

Transfer the mixture to an ice cream machine and churn for 40 minutes. Store in a freezerproof container in the freezer for up to 2 months.

FROZEN GREEK YOGURT

This is a delicious, healthy alternative to ice cream. It goes wonderfully with our quince in syrup instead of the Greek yogurt mousse (see page 217), which is how we like to serve it at MAZI over the summer months.

1 lb 2 oz (500 g) Greek yogurt
6¾ oz (190 ml) milk
6¾ oz (190 g) superfine sugar
1¼ oz (35 g) powdered milk
1¼ oz (35 g) corn syrup
3 tablespoons heavy cream

SERVES 8–10

Put all the ingredients, except the cream, in the bowl of a stand mixer fitted with the paddle attachment and beat on medium-high speed. While the mixer is running, add the cream in a slow, steady stream and mix until well blended.

Transfer the mixture to an ice cream machine and churn for 30–40 minutes. Store in a freezerproof container in the freezer for up to 2 months.

GREEK COFFEE ICE CREAM

3½ oz (100 g) ground
   Greek coffee
7 oz (200 ml) water
19 oz (550 ml) milk
3 oz (85 ml) heavy cream
4¼ oz (120 g) egg yolks
7 oz (200 g) superfine sugar

SERVES 4

Put the Greek coffee and measured water in a saucepan and bring to a boil, stirring. Pass through a fine-mesh strainer, making sure there is no coffee powder left in the infusion, then discard the coffee residue.

Heat a saucepan over medium heat, add the coffee infusion, milk and cream and bring to a boil, stirring.

Meanwhile, put the egg yolks and sugar in the bowl of a stand mixer fitted with the whisk attachment and whisk on medium speed until pale and fluffy. While the mixer is running, pour in the warm coffee mixture and continue mixing until the mixture thickens slightly.

Pour the mixture into a bowl, cover with plastic wrap and leave to cool in the refrigerator. Transfer to an ice cream machine and churn for 40 minutes. Store in a freezerproof container in the freezer for up to 2 months.

Cocktail making using Greek liquor has flourished to become a serious science in Athens, with Greek mixologists taking the world by storm, winning top international competitions with their creativity. In fact, it's fair to say that the Greek bar, whether in the capital, Thessaloniki or Mykonos, has evolved even further than the Greek kitchen in recent times.

At MAZI, we were the first establishment in London to introduce an all-Greek wine and cocktail list, since, as with our food, we wanted to change people's perceptions of the Greek imbibing experience. And as with our food menu, we wanted our cocktail list to reflect the essential character and flavor of Greece by featuring authentic Greek ingredients, but then putting them together in our unique, contemporary MAZI way. And when creating our concoctions, we had in mind all those memorable days and nights back home, partying on the beach or under the stars, so that our guests may sip and share in those good times too.

Our cocktails can be enjoyed before or after dinner as well as with our food.

COCKTAILS

MASTIHA MOJITO

By bringing a Greek twist to this classic, we created our restaurant's most famous cocktail, which has since been recreated by numerous other restaurants and bars. Summers in our garden in Notting Hill are made of this. Just one sip and you will be transported to those wild days and nights on the party island of Mykonos. See the photograph opposite (left).

½ lime
5 mint leaves, plus 2 extra
    to garnish
1 oz (25 ml) sugar syrup
    (see page 14)
2 oz (50 ml) mastiha liqueur
3½ oz (100 ml) soda water
8 ice cubes, crushed

SERVES 1

Cut the lime into 4 pieces and add to a tumbler, or jelly jar if you have one, with the mint leaves and sugar syrup and crush with a muddler.

Add the mastiha liqueur, soda water and crushed ice and stir to mix. Serve with 2 straws, garnished with the extra mint leaves.

TZATZIKI MARTINI

Don't be misled by the name of this cocktail — there is no garlic, yogurt or olive oil in it, just lots of cucumber! Cooling and refreshing, this is perfect on a warm summer's day and has proved to be one of our most celebrated cocktails, loved by customers and critics alike. See the photograph opposite (right).

1 oz (30 g) unpeeled cucumber,
    plus 1 slice to serve
2 oz (50 ml) mastiha liqueur
1 oz (25 ml) gin
juice of ½ lemon
6–8 ice cubes
dill frond, to decorate

SERVES 1

Cut the cucumber into 4 pieces and add to a Boston shaker with the remaining ingredients. Shake really well so that the cucumber disintegrates.

Pour through a mesh strainer into a Martini glass, add the slice of cucumber to enhance the cucumber flavor, decorate with a dill frond and serve immediately.

LEMON MAZI

Tangy and citrusy, this cocktail resonates with the scent and taste of the renowned lemons of the extensive groves on the island of Poros just off the Peloponnese coast.

2 oz (50 ml) vodka
1 oz (25 ml) triple sec
juice of ½ lime
juice of ½ lemon
1 oz (25 ml) sugar syrup
 (*see* page 14)
5 ice cubes
thick lemon twist, to garnish

SERVES 1

Add all the ingredients to a Boston shaker and shake well.

Pour through a strainer into a Champagne glass, garnish with the lemon twist and serve immediately.

LOST IN PAXOS

1 oz (25 ml) ouzo
1 oz (25 ml) vodka
1 oz (25 ml) mastiha liqueur
juice of ½ lemon
1 oz (25 ml) sugar syrup
   (*see* page 14)
5 ice cubes, plus 3, crushed,
   to serve
1 oz (25 ml) soda water
thick lemon twist, to garnish

SERVES 1

This brings together two of Greece's defining alcoholic drinks, both aromatic in their different ways — the famous aniseed-flavored ouzo and the herbaceous-tasting mastiha liqueur — for a heady Hellenic experience.

Add the ouzo, vodka, mastiha liqueur, lemon juice, sugar syrup and ice cubes to a Boston shaker and shake well.

Pour into an Old Fashioned tumbler without straining, add the crushed ice and soda water and stir to mix. Garnish with the lemon twist and serve immediately.

FOUND IN SPETSES

2 oz (50 ml) vodka
1 oz (25 ml) mastiha liqueur
juice of ½ lime
1 oz (25 ml) store-bought
   passion fruit coulis or purée
   (*see* page 14)
4 teaspoons sugar syrup
   (*see* page 14)
5 ice cubes, plus 3, crushed,
   to serve
½ passion fruit, to garnish

SERVES 1

Here, the sweet yet tart, aromatic flavor of the passion fruit pairs perfectly with the fresh, piney notes of the mastiha liqueur to create an exotic-tasting cocktail. What you lost in Paxos will be found on tasting this delicious drink.

Add all the ingredients, except the crushed ice, to a Boston shaker and shake well.

Pour into an Old Fashioned tumbler without straining, add the crushed ice and garnish with the passion fruit half. Serve immediately.

CHIOS MANDARIN MARTINI

juice of 1 mandarin
2 oz (50 ml) vodka
1 oz (25 ml) gin
5 ice cubes
thick mandarin twist,
   to garnish

SERVES 1

In addition to mastiha, the island of Chios is also renowned for producing the best-quality mandarins in Greece, which provided the inspiration for this classy cocktail. See the photograph opposite (left).

Add all the ingredients to a Boston shaker and shake well.

Pour through a strainer into a Martini glass, garnish with the mandarin twist and serve immediately.

COSMOPOLIS

2 oz (50 ml) mastiha liqueur
1 oz (25 ml) vodka
2 oz (50 ml) watermelon juice
juice of ½ lime
splash of sugar syrup
   (*see* page 14)
5 ice cubes

SERVES 1

This vibrantly colored and flavored cocktail has its origins in the watermelon Martini. But we've given it a uniquely Greek edge with the addition of mastiha liqueur made using the aromatic resin of the mastiha tree from the island of Chios (see page 241). See the photograph opposite (right).

Add all the ingredients to a Boston shaker and shake well.

Pour through a strainer into a Martini glass and serve immediately.

GINGEROUZO

Adrien came up with this recipe one day during a very busy service. People loved it and so it became a permanent item on our cocktail list. It's perfect for winter.

2 oz (50 ml) vodka
1 oz (25 ml) ouzo
1 oz (25 ml) freshly squeezed
    orange juice
4 teaspoons sugar syrup
    (*see* page 14)
pinch of salt
small slice of fresh root ginger,
    peeled, plus an extra slice
    to garnish
5 ice cubes, plus 3, crushed,
    to serve

SERVES 1

Add all the ingredients, except the crushed ice, to a Boston shaker and shake well.

Pour through a strainer into an Old Fashioned tumbler and add the crushed ice. Garnish with the extra slice of ginger and serve immediately.

HOT MÉLI

2 oz (50 ml) Metaxa 5, 7 or 12
    star brandy (or other brandy)
1 oz (25 ml) Southern Comfort
1 oz (30 g) honey
juice of ½ lime
thick lime twist, to garnish

SERVES 1

Translating directly from the Greek as hot "honey," this drink was inspired by old wives' cold remedies. We promise you, it really does work as a gentle decongestant and winter warmer on a chilly day.

Combine all the ingredients in a small saucepan over low heat and heat just until the mixture starts sizzling.

Remove from the heat, then pour into a snifter glass, garnish with the lime twist and serve immediately.

MASTIHA DAIQUIRI

juice of ½ lime, plus extra for
    rimming the glass
mastiha powder or
    confectioners sugar,
    for rimming the glass
2 oz (50 ml) mastiha liqueur
1 oz (25 ml) golden rum
splash of sugar syrup
    (see page 14)
8 ice cubes

SERVES 1

For another Greek take on an ever-popular cocktail form, the rum-and-citrus-based Daiquiri, we have introduced a freshening breath of the Aegean in the shape of the digestif, mastiha liqueur (see page 14).

First prepare your glass. Put some lime juice on a saucer and some mastiha powder or confectioners sugar on a second saucer. Turn the rim of a Daiquiri or Martini glass first in the lime juice and then in the mastiha powder or confectioners sugar to coat.

Add all the remaining ingredients to a Boston shaker and shake well.

Pour through a strainer into the prepared glass and serve immediately.

PHILOSYKOS

This cocktail takes its name from a famous perfume by Diptyque with the scent of figs that translates from the Greek as "the one that likes figs." It may sound surprising given our location in London, but we have a beautiful fig tree in our little garden in Notting Hill that actually produces figs of eating quality. One day a customer asked us to make a cocktail for her using our own figs, and this was the delectable result.

You can buy ready-made fig purée (such as Boiron frozen fig purée) from online specialist food suppliers.

2 oz (50 ml) golden rum
1 oz (25 ml) gin
1 oz (25 ml) ready-made
    fig purée
2 teaspoons sugar syrup
    (*see* page 14)
1 drop of lime juice
5 ice cubes, plus 3, crushed,
    to serve
1 fresh fig, halved, to garnish
    (when available)

SERVES 1

Add all the ingredients, except the crushed ice, to a Boston shaker and shake well.

Pour through a strainer into an Old Fashioned tumbler, add the crushed ice and garnish with the fig halves, if available. Serve immediately.

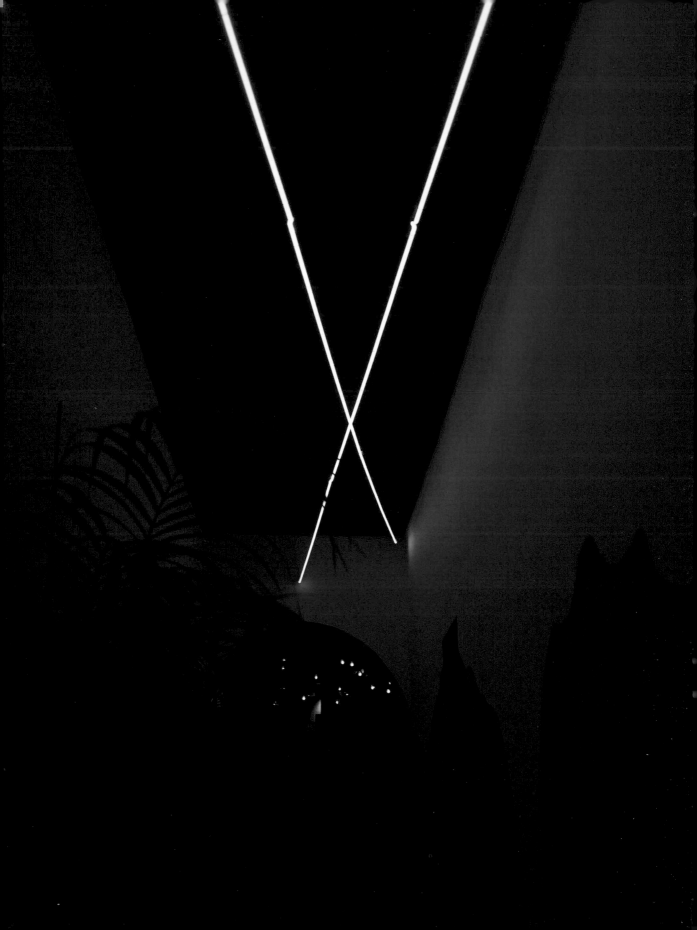

INDEX